SKILLS FOR INVESTING MONEY

EVERYONE SHOULD LEARN
THE SKILLS TO CHANGE
MINDSET AND INVEST MONEY,
FOR PERSONAL AND BUSINESS
SUCCESS. INCLUDING USEFUL
TIPS AND EXERCICES FOR
PERSONAL GROWTH

Table of Contents

Introduction 3

Chapter 1: Mindset 13

Chapter 2: Skills for Changing Mindset............22

Chapter 3: Set Goal..32

Chapter 4: Study and Learn More Skills 44

Chapter 5: Skills for Investing Money...............54

Chapter 6: Personal Success............................64

Chapter 7: Be Successful in Business 74

Chapter 8: Change Lifestyle..............................84

Chapter 9: Train Your Memory........................94

Chapter 10: Never Give Up 105

Chapter 11: Self-Discipline 115

Chapter 12: Meet People of your Same Level . 126

Chapter 13: Plan your Time 136

Conclusion.. 147

Introduction

Investment is a complex subject. Otherwise, everyone would have known about it and be able to do it. If everyone actually knew about investments, then it won't be a place just for the rich, it would be for everyone.

That's why, as you are learning about investments, you should also learn about financial intelligence. The two go hand in hand. So, what are investments, or what does "investing" mean?

Well, investing means a lot of things to different people. For some people, it means buying shares in a profitable company and then maybe selling when the company stocks rise. For some others, it is the buying of mutual funds, and for others, it is buying jewelry and selling later. Some buy mutual funds or treasury bills. Others would buy a piece of land, keep it for a while and then flip it for profits.

Investing involves the acquisition of an asset or goods with the aim that it would appreciate or generate income in the future. These assets or portfolios are usually for the future, could be short term or long term). These investments could be in stock, companies, real estate, or even in one's education or in his/her children. So, investments could actually come in different shades and sizes. Generally speaking, though investments are not only related to money, Investments also can be in terms of time, effort, goodwill and of course, money, in an expectation for high returns in the future. An investor is someone who creates or seeks investment opportunities. Investors make their money work for them.

Investing is one of the easiest ways of becoming financially independent or financially free. There are types of investors and also types of investments one can do; however, before we get there, let's see about financial freedom.

Why Everyone Should Be an Investor

There certain people who don't work, but they earn more than a lot of people who work. One very popular person is Robert Kiyosaki, he retired at 47, and he had investments, which were earning him lots of money, enough money for him to continue to live his lifestyle, without having to work. Another popular guy is Warren Buffet; in fact, he made his money from investments, especially in the stock market. Here are a few reasons why you should invest.

1. Increase your Money

Investments make your money work for you. That way, you're even able to get richer quicker. You are working and then your money is also working for you. Basically, these are actually the only two ways to make money in our world at the moment. You work for money (self-employed, employee or business owner). And then your money works for you, in terms of assets, stocks, bonds and many more.

2. Take Advantages of Tax "Loopholes"

One of the ways for this is to reduce the amount of your income that can be taxed. There are certain kinds of investments, which you can do with pretax money. For example, 401(k), especially those sponsored by employers, can be funded with pretax dollars. Investing from a corporation account also sometimes qualifies you to invest using pretax dollars.

3. Savings for Retirement

Some people just open an account and keep on stashing money in it for their retirement. This is not a bad thing; at least it's better than not saving at all. However, stashing money somewhere might not be the best way to save for your retirement. This is due to inflation. However, to fight against this, money should be an investment. Usually, at a younger age, it is advised that one puts retirement funds in high-risk investment portfolios because they give high yields. And as one gets closer to retirements, lower-risk investments should be considered.

4. Being Part Sometime New

Certain people are called angel investors; they look for startups or people with ideas and try to fund those businesses in the bid to make money. Sometimes, these startups can make an investor so much more, sometimes more than a 1000% profit. For Jason Njoku, the CEO of Iroko TV, a Nigerian startup claimed to have made his investors more than 100% profit. Of course, one doesn't have to be an angel investor to help float a business.

5. Leave an Inheritance

This is another way that parents leave an inheritance for their children. Sometimes an asset is bought in the name of the child or money is put in a particular venture and leaving it until a child gets to a certain age.

6. Hit Financial Goals

Investing is one-way people use in hitting their financial goals. If the venture you invested in turns out to be profitable, there'll be more money.

Skills for Investing Money

When it comes to investing, you must not only think about your short-term goals but must also consider your long-term goals. You not only have to live in your present but must plan for a future too. If you want to start planning the future, then long-term investing is the best option available. However, there are certain tried and tested strategies that you can use to increase your wealth in the long run. In this segment, you will learn about certain tips that you can use for long-term investing.

Top-Performers

A lot of seasoned investors believe that having a couple of top-performing stocks in their investment portfolio can make a major difference. It is a common belief that most of the payout is usually from a couple of investments that are in the mix. Your investment portfolio might include various assets and different investments, but not all of them will perform equally. There will always be certain vendors who provide great returns and whose value keeps increasing. So, spend some time, do some research, and identify the top performers and quickly add them to your portfolio. It is a process of trial and error. It is a good idea to hire the services of a broker who can provide you with sound financial advice. However, please remember that the final decision lies in your hands, and you must do your due diligence before investing.

Get Rid of the bad ones

While you are investing, you will come across certain good and bad stocks, which are a part of your portfolio. If you notice that certain investments aren't doing well or are performing poorly, then get rid of them. A common mistake made by a lot of investors is that they allow such sales to hurt their psyche. It's better to get rid of any poor performers right away instead of allowing them to cause any financial damage. Please remember that a good investor not only knows when to get into the game, but he also knows when to quit. Remember the age-old adage, "a stitch in time saves nine." Well, this is precisely what you must do if you want to build a profitable portfolio. At times, investors tend to base their investment decisions based on any hot tips they get. Please refrain from doing this. If you want to be a successful investor, then you must do the necessary research along with the due diligence before making an investment.

Long-Term Vision

You must concentrate on the bigger picture. It is important to monitor the way your investments perform. However, if you keep constantly checking an investment's performance every minute, it will merely make you panic. To stay interested in your investments, it is quintessential to focus on the bigger picture. Please remember that any volatility in the stock market is only momentary. The investments you made will experience certain fluctuations in their performance. To ensure that your investment portfolio performs well, you must have a combination of short-term as well as long-term instruments. By having a combination of such investments, you can ensure that you will not only be earning profits in the foreseeable future, but we'll keep doing so in the long run too.

Metrics Matter

If you want to become a successful investor, it is quintessential that you start learning about the different metrics involved in financial markets. Learning to analyze metrics will help understand the way a particular investment is towing. Not just that, it will also help you make better decisions. For instance, the price/earnings ratio or the P/E ratio is one of the most important ratios you must consider. By calculating this ratio, you can quickly decide the value of an instrument. That said, there are other factors that you must consider before deciding the value of an investment. There are different factors that influence the value of an investment. You need to thoroughly go through all of those factors along with the necessary metrics for deciding whether an investment will be profitable or not.

Avoid Penny Stocks

A lot of investors think that investing in penny stocks is a quick way to get rich. Penny stocks are extremely volatile. It is rather difficult to predict the way a penny stock will perform. There can be instances when the value of a penny stock can go from $5 to $1. If that happens, you end up losing most of your capital. Therefore, it is a good idea to stay away from penny stocks. If you do want to invest in penny stocks, then make sure that you invest in small amounts. Never risk more than you can afford to lose.

Strategy

Well, there are different strategies that you can use. The one thing that you must understand is that there is no right or wrong way to go about investing. A strategy that might have worked for someone might not work for you. Also, ensure that you aren't too rigid about the investment strategies you use. Be flexible and make the necessary changes as you go along. Once you start investing, you will gain practical experience with the do and don'ts of the financial markets. Allow your knowledge and experience to guide you along the way. Don't be too stuck up on following a specific strategy while investing.

Keep Learning

Information is your ally in the field of investing. Keep learning and never give up an opportunity to learn. Try to be a sponge and keep an open mind about investing. When you start learning about the intricacies of the financial market, you may come across some tips that can come in handy. When you are armed with the right information, it will become easier to make better decisions.

Chapter 1:

Mindset

A positive mindset while at work has a plethora of benefits on your career. It influences the way you handle tasks, the way you think, and also improves the way your employees/colleagues/customers see you.

Your reality is a product of your thought. According to a famous Motivational quote by Henry Ford, founder of Ford Motors, "if you believe you can land a sale, your confidence will shine through, and raise the possibility of you performing well and making the sale."

Therefore, you need to apply the principles of positive thinking to maximize your potentials at work. Here are some of the things to expect when you combine positive thinking with your career:

Reduced Stress

Having a positive mindset lets you reframe problems as minor setbacks rather than a cause for stress. At the end of each day, you'll leave work feeling accomplished and happy that you overcame all the professional challenges with a smile.

Improved Productivity

Also, thinking positively, let's tackles tasks quickly, thus raising your efficiency, especially if it's a demanding job. Your brain thinks clearly, and your energy levels are high, which makes you adequately equipped - mentally - to complete tasks.

The reduced stress levels also help clear your mind and raise your ability to focus, listen, and reply appropriately; you become a better communicator.

Better Problem-Solving Skills

People who are willing to pause and analyze a situation in search of the cause become excellent at solving problems. This ability is essential in every career, whether it be an engineer, pilot, customer service representative, director, nanny, etc.

Skill Acquisition

A positive mindset will detach you from an unhealthy ego and open your mind to receive help or master new skills from your co-workers or formal training programs. You'll also have the courage to try new things because you believe in a positive outcome.

Better Decision-Making

Without stress or fear blocking your ability to focus, you will have the power to make better and intelligent decisions at work. This improvement will directly result in a boost in confidence in the fact that you're making the right decisions.

Quickly Recognize Opportunities

Going through work with confidence and a stress-free mind will give you the conviction to seize opportunities like training programs and promotions because you feel comfortable outside your comfort zone. You will treat prospects as an avenue for advancement, rather than a threat to your currently perceived comfort.

Taking advantage of opportunities increases your chance of career success, unlike stay in the same.

Increased Resilience

Although having a positive mindset doesn't mean everything will go the way you plan, however, it helps you critically analyze your situation and take actionable steps towards success.

The benefits associated with having a positive mindset in your career are virtually endless but undeniably profitable.

How to Think Positively at Work

Changing your attitude towards corporate stress from a negative perspective to a positive one is a habit that will undoubtedly benefit your profession. Although the same techniques for positive thinking might not work on all types of individuals, the ones listed below are guaranteed to guide your transition from negativity to positivity.

Below are a few steps to help you remain positive at work:

- **Recognize your Thoughts**

Take some time - in the shower or while you eat - and replay your thoughts throughout the day. For example, you attended a meeting with someone you think has an inadequate personality, what was your first thought about that person? If it were negative, then make a mental commitment to avoid thinking negatively about people and labeling them as good or bad.

- **Stay Healthy**

The well-being of your body is essential to your mind. Therefore, you need to take care of yourself by getting approximately 8 hours of sleep, eating a balanced diet, and exercising frequently.

Making this routine into a daily habit will boost your energy and give you the mental space to accommodate problems and produce solutions.

- **Be Active**

One suitable method to nourish a healthy mindset is to engage in activities that improve your mood. These activities include sports, yoga, hobbies, meditation, and parties with friends, etc. Whatever makes you feel good?

As long as you build a healthy mindset with these activities, you will stay optimistic at work.

Cultivate Relationships with Positive People

A section in the Christian Bible says, "a man builds the countenance of his friend just the way iron sharpens iron." therefore, keeping a circle of optimistic friends who also believe in positive thinking, is a sure-fire way to stay motivated throughout the day.

- **Change what you Can**

No, everything in your environment will respond the way you expect. So, direct your attention to factors within your control; become a problem solver. However, if the situation has no remedy, remember the event as a lesson and use it to improve yourself.

- **Accept your Errors**

One problem most optimists face at work is the depression they feel after getting 5he boss scolds then for a mistake. Although the talk might hurt on an emotional level, don't take the pain to heart. Instead, accept your error, learn the lesson, and commit to doing better in the future.

Maintaining a positive mindset at work is often challenging, especially when stress and disappointment are the office's norms. Fortunate, the strategies above are timeless, and they will help you overcome the daily corporate hurdles with a smile.

Factors that Ruin your Mood at Work

It's essential to have a good understanding of what ruins your day at work so that you can expect or avoid them. Without this knowledge, you might get stuck or fail to stay optimistic throughout the day.

Anyway, here's a quick rundown of the factor that contributes to a bad day at work:

- **Inadequate Sleep**

The primary cause of poor performance at work is usually a lack of sleep. Although doctors agree that humans need at least eight hours of sleep, some people can survive with less.

However, ensure you go to bed early and get the recommended night's rest. You can set the alarm to remind you an hour before bedtime, so you remain punctual.

Remember, a healthy mind is the fuel of optimism.

- **Poor Clothing**

You're bound to ruin your day if your clothes are the wrong fit, look unkempt, or smell terrible. You will end up feeling uncomfortable, self-conscious, and a lack of self-esteem, which leads to nourishing negative thoughts and manifest failure.

- **Bad Company**

Whether it's your friend, family member, boss, employee, or customers, people with a negative perspective on life tend to drain others of energy. If such people are at your place of work, you try to limit the level of closure they have with you, so they won't infect your mind with negativity and corrupt your developing optimism.

- **Overworking**

Working extra hours in your job or business might get you some praise or fleeting gratification, but the result is a poor physical and mental stamina. Eventually, you will be unable to fulfill orders or solve problems optimistically.

Ensure you get some sleep and finish your daily tasks before the end of the workday.

- **Social Media**

Recent studies suggest that spending too much time on social media contributes to the feeling of boredom. Not only will you feel tied down, but consistent use of social media will waste your time, leaving you feeling guilty of procrastination.

Therefore, spend time with your colleagues when you're bored or free, and have a live conversation, instead of scrolling all day on Instagram.

Making a conscious effort to avoid the factors listed above is a step further in maintaining a positive mindset at work. Remember, a positive mindset is an essential tool for career advancement.

Chapter 2:

Skills for Changing Mindset

Before you change the world around you, you must first change yourself. First, we'll learn how to believe in yourself so that you can face your fears. Once you get out of your comfort zone and realize that you have unlimited potential, then it will be easy for you to determine your life goals.

Unfortunately, not all of our goals and dreams are achieved right away. That's why it's important to cultivate inner patience and to strive for inner peace and compassion. Once you've achieved that, then you will understand what your focus should be on any given day. When you combine a strong focus with a large dream for your life, then you can achieve everything you want

Face your Fear

Your fears will not go away unless you face them! If you really want to expand your mind, you should be driven to do the things that scare you. There are a few things that happen when you go out on a limb and do the things that you're afraid of. First, you start to understand the misconceptions that people have about different cultures, religions, and geographical locations. Second, you expand your mind and learn that you can achieve even the things that might make you scared. Third, you expand your potential and start thinking differently because of the unique experiences that you've had.

So how do you face your fears? Here are all of the different steps you can take to turn your fears into your passions…

I. Understand that everyone has fears. Acknowledge the things that you're afraid of without feeling embarrassed or beating yourself up.
II. Write down your fears. Do you know why you are scared of these things? Make sure that

whenever you overcome a fear that you wrote on this list, that you cross it off and share your new thought process on another piece of paper.

III. Are some of your fears reasonable? Some things are really scary, and rightfully so! Those really scary things that are on your list because they're really dangerous don't have to be changed. But what about your irrational fears? Determine which ones are rational and which ones are irrational, and then start changing your mindset on your irrational fears.

IV. Break down your irrational fears. Take things slowly and break down your irrational fears into smaller tasks. For instance, if you have a fear of heights, don't go to the top of the Eiffel Tower first thing! Start by going hiking to a beautiful viewpoint, taking a glass elevator to the top floor of a shopping center, or just climbing a play structure at a playground.

Once you've done all the little tasks on your list, then you can try and concur with your bigger fears by sitting on a Ferris wheel, going for a hot-air balloon ride, or even by skydiving! You might just find something that you're passionate about.

V. Live in the moment. While you're tackling your fears, don't worry about the future, which has not yet arrived. Focus on your breathing, relax your body, and bring yourself to the present moment.

VI. Consider your past accomplishments. That's right; you've likely done something that's even scarier or something that has led you to dispel your fear. Just remember how amazing it was to get over your previous fear so that you could push yourself even more at this very moment. When you've experienced new areas of the world and discovered new passions by believing in yourself and facing your fears, then it's time to determine your life goals.

Determine your Life Purpose

What brings you happiness? What fills you with joy and passion? Think about this for a second. Perhaps you have all these things that you love, but you fail to make any progress toward achieving them because of all the other tasks that you have to accomplish each day. It's okay because you're not alone! You can start living a more fulfilling life by finding your passion by determining your life's purpose. Here's how:

I. Keep a journal. Hopefully, you have already done this to list down your past accomplishments and to keep track of the fears that you've eliminated. Now it's time to take that journal and write down why you think you're on Earth, the things in life that your passionate about, and what brings you joy.

II. Dive deeper into your interests. Discuss the times where you have been truly happy. Write about the people who are most interesting to you. Discuss how you like to spend your time. Do you have any role models? What would you do if you only had one week to live? These prompts will help you determine the things that you are truly passionate about so that you can fill more of your time with that.

III. Discuss the people and places that you love. This will explain where your heart lies while bringing you closer to learning about the life you want to live. What would you be doing if you had no limitations? When you focus on what you love, you uncover passions that go deeper than the things that you value with reason.

IV. Plan backward. What would your ideal life be from 100 years old to now? How would you spend your time? What things would you achieve? Write down everything you want to do in order to live a life of passion. Somewhere in the process is your life passion.

Allow yourself to Be Patient

The most successful people do the work that they need to when they need to do it, but they also understand that it isn't possible to do everything. Everyone has to rely on someone else for something, and not everything always goes to plan the minute that you want it to. That's why it's important to cultivate patience. Patience is what will allow you to find new opportunities, live all of your passions, and adopt a positive mindset. Here are three things to consider while building your patience:

I. Waiting makes you happier. That's right, and it has been scientifically proven that if you wait for something, you value it more. Sure, it's really nice to be instantly gratified.

II. Patience allows new opportunities to come into your life. The longer that you can wait for the perfect opportunity, the easier it will be for you to achieve greatness when the time is right. Right now, it might not be the best time to invest, purchase a home, or accomplish all of your dreams. That's all right! Soon new opportunities will present themselves if you're patient, and you'll benefit from waiting until the time is right.

III. Patience changes your perception of yourself and others. It's easy to be hard on yourself or to demand that other people are perfect while in your company. The problem is that no one (yourself included) is perfect! Have patience with people and believe that they can complete what they say they will. Give them enough time to be creative, and they'll come through for you. On the same note, give yourself the time to develop fully into the person that you want to be as well.

IV. When you live a life of patience, you're able to fully develop your skills and wait until the time is right. You see people differently and are more willing to be fluid instead of ridged. Success comes to people who are accommodating. You can find success in life if you are patient with yourself and reasonable with your expectation of others.

Learn how to Focus

Developing more focus will allow you to achieve more and it will also make you a happier person! When you stop focusing on the things that no longer benefit you and instead concentrate just on what will help you accomplish the goals and dreams that you have, then you'll be able to accomplish your goals. It's not always easy to reduce distractions, but if you learn how to, then you'll be able to achieve more in a day, then you thought possible. Here's how to increase your focus:

I. Concentrate on one thing at a time. Start by focusing on accomplishing one task for thirty minutes. At this time, don't listen to music, browse your Facebook, or check your cell phone. Just make progress toward whatever you're trying to accomplish. When the initial time has passed, continue with your task and push yourself to see how long you can keep your focus.

As time goes on, you'll build your focus. Remember, everyone needs a break of at least 7 minutes per hour of work, so when you start working for longer periods of time, then make sure that you rest. Do whatever you want on your break and then come back to work promptly, again avoiding distractions. Soon you'll achieve your goals without concentrating on any of the other things that waste your time.

II. Meditate daily. Sit in silence in a comfortable position for a few minutes each day. Every day, push yourself to meditate for a longer period of time until you can sit for 20 minutes comfortably. Relax and focus on your breathing while allowing any thoughts that you have to come and pass. Once you've finished, take some time to come back to your senses before getting up. This will improve your concentration and focus throughout the rest of the day if you make it a daily habit.

III. Know what you're going to do a day before you do it. That's right, keeping a to-do list is the best way to make sure that you achieve your goals. When you know what it is that you want to accomplish each day, then you will spend more time actually achieving your daily goals. Without a to-do list, you're more likely to float around from one thing to the next without actually accomplishing anything.

Once you've learned how to concentrate, determined your goals, defined your life purpose, and understand how to be patient, and then you can determine your dream.

Chapter 3:

Set Goal

Set big goals and work smarter to achieve them. When you hit your first goal, set another higher goal, and keep on setting goals until you hit the stars. I would rather set the highest goals of my life and fail than not setting any goals at all.

One thing I have learned after 20 years of experience managing multi-million-pound UK businesses, consulting in Higher Education, Police Training Academy, Housing Estates, advisor to heads of Schools, business owners, 1-2-1 business mentoring, and reading so many books on the biographies of entrepreneurs, young and old, and how they rose from rags-to-riches is nothing other than setting ambitious goals they could ever imagine.

The questions I would like to ask you are these: What is your ultimate goal in starting your own business? Is it to make money, or to solve a problem in society? Is it not better for you to be employed by other companies to drive their own strategies, so they pay you a salary in return for your time?

If your ultimate goal is to make money and become rich, this step would allude to you. The more you chase money, the more it runs away, and you will ultimately find yourself in a cycle of rat-race. You will become a slave to money. This mental attitude could lead you into illicit businesses just because you want to be rich just like your peers. Do not work for the sake of earning money; rather, let money work for you in a business you are passionate about.

However, if your ultimate goal in business is to solve a particular problem in the society, be it in fashion, food, medicines, etc., by discovering unique goods and services that people value most, like precious metals such as silver and gold, are valued, no matter where you are in the world, people will seek your services with their money and find you. Your valued offerings attract valued customers who want to spend their valued money on you, and your goods or services.

As a proud business owner, you will suddenly become a business strategist, a fortune teller, or soothsayer. Your ambition is to translate your company's vision into specifically defined goals and back up your wisdom with the step-by-step guide on "the technical know-how" to achieve those goals.

Have your Goals & Plans Written Down

You should always have your ideas or goals written down. On average, the human brain is constantly processing about 23 words per second or 34 Gigabytes of data per day – which is an equivalent volume of data required to overload or kill off a laptop in seven days (Andrea 2016).

So, the chances are that not everything you ever discoursed or planned to do would ever be remembered. By forming a habit of jotting down your ideas, your goals, or your plans, you have the privilege of going back to the same pieces of information the same way you wrote them.

With thousands upon thousands of messages we read every day, ranging from emails to letters, newsletters, phone calls, text messages, internet, social media, radios, TVs, newspapers, etc., our brain is inundated with information that it cannot retain.

The importance of writing things down for the sake of posterity – was amplified in the Holy Bible. As I searched the scriptures to enrich myself with knowledge on why God placed so much value on having goals written down, I concluded that the act or art of writing goals or targets down has a divine connection with God.

These mind-boggling statistics make too much sense to be untrue. They are, in fact, false and fake news and were debunked by various authors to be untrue. According to Lawrence Tabak, in 1996, these statistics were used by some of the well-known Inspirational speakers, Zig Ziglar's, successful videos, etc. to spike enthusiasm in their target audiences.

On 1st January 2020 while writing this guidebook – Starting a Successful £1Million Business, I decided to Google "Yale Written Goals Study or Harvard Written Goals Study" without the quotation marks. I was shocked to find 7,030,000 hits written about the studies.

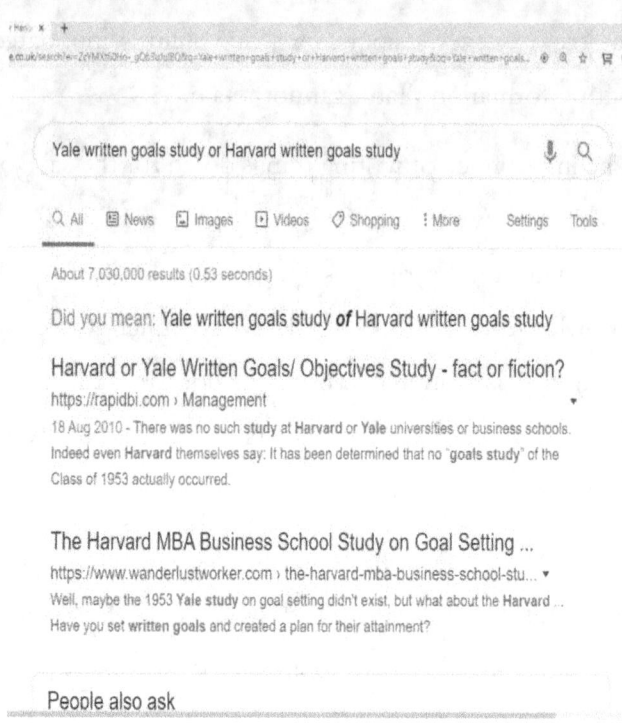

Google Internet Search Results

Unfortunately, despite the popularity of these statistics, they are not real. I first stumbled into these stories during my Executive MBA programmed. Although they are fake, it is sensible for us to jot down our goals. Whatever we do in our personal lives, in business, family, marriage, etc. It is imperative to write our goals and plans down in black and white, so we do not forget them in the future. In the next 3-6 months, you might want to go back to your notepad, review your entries, and evaluate if you are working within the confinement of your set goals.

Breakdown your Goals

While the importance of writing down your ideas cannot be overemphasized, it is vital to set goals that are achievable and break them down bit-by-bit, and chunk-by-chunk. I have always told my children that Mathematics is the easiest subject to master if you know the secret - breaking down the components of each question bits-by-bits and chunk-by-chunk.

The same principle is applicable in the business and financial world. For instance, if your goal is to make £1Million-pound GBP revenue in one year to two years, you have to break down your targets into months and work downwards into weeks and days. This enables you to know exactly how much your business needs to make to reach that goal or to break-even, and if your target is achievable.

There is no need to swim in the ocean without a direction; otherwise, you will be swept away by the tide. The same is applicable in business. You must decide how much you have to make and devise compelling and robust strategies to beat your target.

For the example we had given on the previous page, to make a one-million-pound turnover in 12 months, you should aim at making £20,000 on sales per week, or £4,000 per day in a five-day working week. Do not set goals you could not achieve. Do not go into business for the sole aim of making money; rather, aim at providing a unique solution for others.

The money will seek you and find you if you are so unique, so valuable like Gold to differentiate your offerings from the competition. What do you offer differently to convince me to leave my current supplier and choose your goods and services?

Do you have that valued solution most people want, which can attract them to your website, store, or platform, and which your competitors do not currently have? If your objective is to sell cheaper than the competition, it might take you years to reach the threshold of your target.

For instance, if you provide great services or goods which are so unique, distinct, highly regarded or valued around the world, and your price tag is set at £30,000 per consultation, people who know the true worth of your services would seek you and find you.

The honest truth is that, in normal circumstances, these people are not looking for you. Rather, they are looking for your unique services or the unique God-given gifts that no one else could offer except you. It is that unique God-gifts that attract them to you and then pay you a premium to receive those services. That's why consultants are highly paid because of their unique services.

Be Aggressive

Not many clients want someone weak negotiating on their behalf. The word aggressive can sometimes have a negative connotation, but it doesn't have to in this circumstance. Being aggressive means, you treat the deal like it's your own. It means you will stay on top of the other agent to make sure things are done on time. Being aggressive means following up consistently with leads. Being aggressive is asking more and more questions and digging more deeply to get to the real reasons and motivations of your clients. Being aggressive is fighting for every dollar for your client.

I've always been an advocate for owning your own home and also investing in real estate. As someone whose business is to help people buy homes and educate them why it's a smart decision to own their own home, it seems counterintuitive to not want the same for yourself. How can you convince someone else it's such a smart thing to do if you haven't done it yourself? Plus, as an agent, there are so many benefits to buying real estate. 95% of the time you make a commission when you buy properties! That's amazing. You get back 2-3% off of the sales price automatically. And that's even before you begin negotiating the price. It's fantastic.

Know what you Want Rather than what you Don't Want

The most successful people in life know what they want rather than what they don't want. We are aware of spending time with our business partners and mentees that several people find it tough to see their way forward. They know what they don't want to have in their life either in the present or the future, but then up until they know what they do want, it makes it difficult to have a clear plan to make changes. But on the other hand, if you do know what you don't want, it's a good place to start. If you don't want to be out of work, stressed, or fed up with your job go ahead and ask yourself what you want instead.

Enjoy the Journey and the Successes You Have Along the Way

If you are always striving for the next big thing, you will never take time to relish the individual achievements along the way. Take time to concentrate on the things that have gone well and the good things that have happened to you. Just like you would break a large goal down into manageable chunks, do the same with your successes. To set these goals we recommend you need to use the principles of setting smarter goals.

Work-Life Balance

You see, once you start planning out your whole day, you become more aware of your time and how to balance it out. Once you begin to write out your entire day ahead of you, you will know precisely what you are doing that day, so you don't have to do anything sporadically throughout the day. Always plan some time for yourself every day where you can wind down, read a good book, meditate, or maybe hang out with your friends. You will feel refreshed the next day. Having to wind down and "chill out" will only make you a more productive person.

Planning out your whole day ahead will not only help you prioritize better. It will also help you be more focused on your task on hand and will help you have a better work-life balance.

Be Grateful

We will be talking about how to be grateful and what the benefits are of being thankful for what you have! Now, believe it or not, being grateful every day will help you get more things done while keeping your mood elevated. See, when you're thankful for the things you have, you will start to feel like your mind is full of peace and joy. When your mind is in order and comfort, you will be more productive with all the tasks ahead of you that day. Being in a grateful state of mind will help you become less stressed and more positive, which will help your work quality tenfold. So, it is pretty essential that you stay grateful not only for better work performance but also to be in a peaceful state of mind. This will also help you to do more positive things with your Amazon FBA. Let's discuss the three main benefits of being thankful.

Chapter 4:

Study and Learn More Skills

Let's learn skills on how to create a business!

Pick your Niche

Before you even get into the process of building your business, you need to decide what you are going to sell. While some websites like Amazon.com can get away with selling virtually everything, people who are just starting out are better off if they stick to a single niche. Picking a niche gives you the opportunity to identify exactly who your target audience is, and then successfully market towards that audience. While you can expand in the future, you want to start with something smaller and manageable.

There are a few things that go into making a niche that is going to be a success for your business. First, you want to pick a niche that is performing well. It should not be saturated, but it should be big enough that you effectively have the potential to earn a profit from it. Just because a niche is a niche doesn't mean it is a good one. In addition to a niche that performs well, you also want to pick one that you are actually interested in. If you are interested in the niche you are getting involved with; you will have significantly higher success with your business than if you are not interested in it at all. Being interested in the niche you are going to sell it gives you the advantage of having the opportunity to understand what your target audience wants and how you can meet their needs.

To start the process of picking your niche, start by writing down; about 5-10 categories for things that you are interested in and would enjoy selling. From those categories, you can start conducting your research. Find out which ones perform well and which ones don't. Take the ones that do and use these as the basis for further research. Start by going to places like Shopify and Amazon and looking at how these categories perform. Furthermore, take note of who is in the industry already selling products. To be successful in a niche, regardless of how many people are currently selling in it, you need to be able to have a competitive edge. Identifying whether or not you will have a competitive edge will come from doing some research about suppliers. While you certainly don't need to pick one yet, you will want to discover what type of pricing you are going to be offering for various items in each niche. Find one where you can offer comparable and competitive pricing.

Once you have conducted your research, you will likely have one or two niches left that are qualified for a successful business. If you have one, then your choice is clear. However, if you end up with two or three, then you are going to have to decide which one you want to do. If the choice isn't obvious based on niche performance, then you can simply choose which one you would enjoy most. The final answer will be the niche that you are going to build your entire business around. Identify

Your Ideal Market

Assuming you have chosen a niche that you are really interested in, you should have a simple time identifying who your target audience is. Knowing who your target audience is will set you up for the future of your business. Every decision you make will be based on the intention of serving this audience and creating a brand and business that will meet their needs and attract their interest. If you cannot effectively communicate with your target audience, then you are not going to be able to make any sales.

It may seem easier to create a broader audience so that you have more potential reach, but the reality is that this will truly dampen your efforts. In the beginning, you want to be very specific about who your target audience is. Once you have successfully served them, it is likely that others will develop an interest in your business, and you will be able to broaden your audience. However, keep that as an opportunity for future growth and remain clear and focused on one specific ideal consumer for the time being.

When you are preparing to outline your ideal market, start by researching similar companies and who they are targeting. Take notice of exactly who they are focusing on in their ads. Is it families? Single females? Single males? Pre-marital couples? Individuals with specific interests? Get as clear on the exact person that is being targeted as you possibly can. You can also conduct some research by looking into the products themselves. See if you can find the products being discoursed on forums anywhere and take note of the type of people who are engaging in the conversation the most. These are the exact people you are going to want to identify as your ideal audience.

The following list consists of things you should consider when you are targeting customers in your business. If you can answer these questions, then you should be clear on whom you are targeting which will make establishing your business significantly easier:

- What is the age range of your targeted audience?
- Is there a primary gender that appears to be interested in your niche?
- What hobbies do these people have?
- Are there any specific phrases or slang that they use when speaking about this niche?
- How does this particular product category serve their needs?

- Why are they interested in these products?
- Do they have anything else in common, regardless of whether or not it pertains directly to the niche?
- Is there any particular icon, color, logo, or "style" that they tend to be drawn towards?
- What are their current favorite brands? Who are they purchasing products like yours from the most?
- What "feeling" do you get from these people?

When you answer these questions, you make it significantly easier for you to develop your brand. You also make the process of choosing products and marketing easier as well. It is vital that you establish the answers to these questions now as opposed to later. Answering them now can be the defining factor that sets you up for total success in your business overall. It is absolutely vital that you take the time to answer these questions in as much detail as possible. While it can take a bit longer than you may have anticipated, it can add a tremendous amount of value to your ability to create a sustainable and successful business out of the gate.

Outline a Brand that Serves your Ideal Market

Now is the first time that you are going to put your market research to good use. When you are building your website and marketing your new business, you are going to want to have a specific brand image that you operate under. The market research you have conducted is going to assist you in deciding exactly how you are going to create your brand, what image you are going to portray, and how you should portray it in order to speak to your ideal client. If you are already knowledgeable in your niche and have some level of passion in it, then this should be fairly easy for you. The market research you have conducted should make it even easier.

There is a great deal of detail that goes into creating a brand. You want to make sure that your image is consistent, your vocabulary and language should be consistent, and the "personality" your company gives off should be consistent. Should you ever hire anyone to help you, they should be able to create content for your brand that is consistent with the image that you have created. This way, people will be able to identify your brand and establish a relationship with your business, as they will feel a sense of recognition and trust for the brand you have created.

The first step you should take when creating your brand is considering your image. Your image is created using actual images, colors, and specific designs. Your primary opportunity to create your image is on your website, though you can use social media profiles to emphasize your image as well. In fact, if you have any social media profiles, they should all utilize your brand image to create the consistency that is required to have a strong brand. All of your marketing and ad campaigns should maintain this image as well. Before you start structuring your website and other major projects, start by sitting down and identifying what you want your brand to be. Websites like Pinterest are excellent for choosing brand designs as they offer a series of color palettes and fonts that flow well together. In addition to colors and fonts, you will want to consider actual images. Most brands have a specific symbol that goes along with their brands, such as Nike's checkmark or apple's computer. You should choose a symbol that will be used across your brand as well. Then, you should also choose specific images. If you are selling yoga products, for example, you may wish to use only images that reflect the outdoors, freedom, and holistic wellness primarily through yoga poses and other similar activities.

Once you have created your brand image, you should carry on creating your brand's vocabulary and "personality." Using the catchphrases and vocabulary you identified during your market research process, you should develop a slogan. You should also practice creating content and copy that uses this slang and phrasing to communicate with your targeted audience effectively. Whenever you are posting about your business, you should use this vocabulary and personality-type to communicate with your audience.

Creating a solid brand is vital to the success of your business. In order to have a business that thrives, you need to be able to create a brand that is identifiable and strong. Believe it or not, your brand is a large part of your marketing. If you are able to create a brand that is identifiable, people are going to think about you a lot more frequently. Consider the Apple logo, for example. Whenever someone sees the Apple logo, even if there are no identifiable phrases surrounding the logo, they are well aware of what the logo stands for. The brand has identified itself so successfully that in many cases people even say "Apple" or when they look at an apple, they may subconsciously think of the brand itself. This type of branding provides you with the opportunity to stay relevant and fresh in people's minds. While you will not have this immediately, you should aim for this right from the beginning. Thinking about your future success now is what will set you up to earn a six-figure income through your Drop shipping business.

Chapter 5:

Skills for Investing Money

Creating a Money-Making Portfolio

The main vehicle that you must rely on is investing. You need to create wealth or a semblance of it with the first two and then grow that wealth into something more through investments. Many people have the assumption that investing requires a lot of skills and techniques, so they think only professionals should do it. So, they tend to blindly follow the advice of these so-called professionals whose primary aim is to enrich them. Then they start to lose money to taxes and hidden charges that the investor barely notices because they are still making money. You'd be surprised by the amount of people that have found themselves in this situation.

You can avoid this by taking the time to look behind the mirage created by the investment industry called Wall Street. You will begin to understand that investing is really not as complicated as they make it out to be. You just need to develop a strong portfolio on which you can base your strategy. You want to make money from your investment, and it will be easier to do so if you play to your strengths.

Understanding the Investment Math

Three main factors will determine how successful you will be as an investor. They are:

1. Your principal/how much you are starting with. This depends on how much you can save, which is usually determined by how much you earn and when you started saving.
2. The returns rate on each investment. The higher your return rates, the more money you make and the earlier you can achieve financial independence.
3. The amount of time afforded for investment. This depends on the amount of time you have before you retire. You will have more time and

be able to make more money if you start investing early in your career.

The Passive Method

This is what most people see as traditional investments. It involves buying stocks and bonds at low-costs and watching them grow in value. The money you use to fund this index investing is from your savings. People after financial independence usually have more principal to start with because they save a lot more of their earnings. Your only problem will be how to find what to invest in. It requires minimal effort after this. You can go back to your day job while your money keeps growing.

You will also keep adding more money to your principal as you make more money and save more. The amount of money you can invest will play a vital role in how soon you can achieve financial independence. You can also save a lot of money in the long run by cutting back on expense ratios and financial advisors. This may not take more than 1% of your budget, but that is a lot of money over the course of your career.

You can then add the amount of money you saved to your principal.

Your chance of success depends a lot on the amount of money you can pour into this principal. That is why it isn't really viable for people with low income or anybody who has to pay off debts, because people in both groups would have low savings. You also can't forget that the stock market is like a grand casino. It's a lot like gambling. You have virtually no control over anything. You will be making financial decisions based on past events and future projections, but you have no choice but to accept whatever returns the market generates. The predictions don't offer any certainty. It may not go according to plans, or it may exceed expectations. You have to live with whatever happens. But returns rarely exceed the past, so that maybe just an unlikely dream. However, you can expect a profit of at most 12% per year.

The Active Method

This is about taking charge and investing in a business of your own. It has some advantages over the passive approach since you will have more control over various aspects that determine the returns on your investment. The sky is the limit for you, or should we say, you can go as far as you're willing to. You need to create a service or product that people will be willing to buy. This is an added advantage to this approach because it provides the fulfillment of turning your idea into something of value. You will also be able to make more money and grow faster. The leverage that you can acquire with this approach will increase your earning potential.

Above all, you will be privy to tax advantages that you couldn't access as an employee. Other financial advantages include tax deductibles, tax deferment, and many more incentives that we have already discoursed. It doesn't come without some risks, though. You have to take responsibility for the business, whether it succeeds or fails. For every successful business that you know, there are ten more that didn't get off the ground. This is a high risk, high reward method. You are going for all or nothing, so you need to put in the effort necessary to succeed.

The Hybrid Method

Most people who want financial independence often choose this approach. It involves investing in real estate. It possesses attributes of the two other approaches to invest. It involves investing in and generating interest and dividends stocks and bonds. It is also a source of consistent regular revenue from interests and rental fees. Your main job will be to find the right property, and everything will pretty much take care of itself from there without much active involvement. The value of housing and real estate always increases.

You can start real estate as both a big or small business. You will get many tax incentives and leverages, and you will be able to make an immense profit from sweet equity. After discovering and buying the right property, your next job will be to find the right tenants. While you are actively looking for properties in the first stage, tenants will be the ones coming to you. Your job will be to select the good ones and find a way to identify and weed out bad tenants. This is not too complicated of a job. It is one that you can handle yourself or you can hire someone to do it for you. How well you or your employees perform these tasks will determine how successful your venture will be.

Why you Should Combine the Methods

You may want to select one approach and just stick to it, but you can go a lot faster if you make use of more strategies. However, I get that you don't want to be overwhelmed and there is a way to prevent that. You don't have to use all three strategies at the same time, you can switch to use the one that will be the most effective for each situation. A method you can use is house hacking, in which you buy a building with multi-housing units. You can then rent out other parts of the building to tenants in order to make money. You will also be reducing or virtually eliminating your personal cost of housing. It can be a cheap and small building, but that doesn't matter much if you have people willing to rent. Your tenants will be the ones paying for your housing and you are guaranteed a profit on your investments. You can then save more money so that you will have more principal to invest in passive streams of income like index funds.

If you have the money to buy a better building or you can own a building without having to reside in it, it's even better. You can keep your high earning job while you keep investing in more properties. You will also be saving your money with all the tax incentives available. However, real estate is not the only option to reach financial independence. Investing in index funds is a pretty efficient method as long as you can get enough principal. If you can save about 50% of your earnings and use that money to invest, you should be able to achieve financial independence within ten to fifteen years. Entrepreneurs have an advantage over people who work under an employer because they tend to enjoy the benefits associated with financial independence, long before they actually attain it. This includes the option to work when you want to, and only to take the jobs you want to take. You have total control over your schedule because you don't have to work for anyone.

You will be able to do the things you want to do whenever you want to do them. You can go on that vacation that you've always wanted or stayed at home to spend time with your family. There is nothing like being genuinely interested and passionate about what you are working on. It brings an extra level of motivation and perseverance. Yet, the most important advantage of working for yourself may be the fact that you are solely responsible for the level of growth your business will see.

You can keep growing larger. So far, you are willing to put in the required efforts and resources. The amount of growth you can see on a regular job is limited to the structure put in place by your employer. For income, you may be able to attain up to 1-3% increment in your salary annually, but being an entrepreneur allows you to experience growth on a weekly or even daily basis. You don't even have to leave the security of a regular monthly salary to enjoy these benefits. Many people have come to see the potential in owning a business and how that can quickly bring them closer to achieving financial independence.

Therefore, some may decide to leave their job and focus on being an entrepreneur. You don't need to depend on one option; you can utilize them all to great effect. While you can invest in index funds and make a lot of money, the principal you will use has to come from somewhere. So you can either have a regular job or a business or have both as your source of income. You will then save money from these sources and use them in your investment portfolio. You can see that all the methods can be utilized together or interchangeably.

Chapter 6:

Personal Success

Success is not a single quality, characteristic, or trait. Everyone would be successful if it were a handout. Instead, success is a delicate blended mix of your characteristics and habits. Just like ingredients in a meal, too much confidence, or too little attention to detail, will cause the dish to fall apart. Everyone wants success; nobody's passion is to become a lousy business owner. However, what separates the average from the best? Traits and behaviors identifying them are easy; practicing them is the challenge. Below are the attributes to practice now:

The Right Mindset

Knowing that you owe money is never a good feeling. It can make you feel disheartened and even disappointed. Well, please remember that it is okay to feel bad. People tend to feel quite stressed whenever the topic of money comes up. You must ensure that you have the right mindset about money. You can attain financial independence if you take the right decisions and make the right investments. The major problem is that a lot of people seem to have a negative attitude about money. People tend to associate shame with a lack of money. It is a popular misconception that money is the root of all evil. You cannot ignore the fact that money is quintessential for a reasonable living. However, the problem is that people tend to make is by putting money above anything else. Money is essential, but that must not be your only priority. It certainly helps you acquire things, but it is merely a tool that you can use in life. It isn't your life. So, it is time to change your attitude about money. Once you start viewing it as a tool, which will help accomplish your goal of attaining financial independence, you will have a positive attitude about it. Money is a tool and money is also power; some of the most powerful people in the world are the rich. You should develop an affinity for money. Like money, I dare say you should love it. See it as your friend as an enabler of sorts for the things you'd like to do. And when you begin to like money, your mind can begin working on ideas that would produce your money. In fact, opportunities that you never saw before, you'd begin to see them.

Your thoughts tend to have a lot of influence on your actions. Consciously or subconsciously, the attitude you have about money will guide your decisions in life. So, if you have a negative mindset about money, you might be subconsciously sabotaging your chances of becoming financially independent.

Track our Expenses

Do you usually keep track of your monthly expenses? If you don't, then it's quintessential that you start doing so. You will never be able to save if you don't keep track of your earnings and expenses. There are different applications that you can use to keep track of your monthly spending. If not, you can always maintain a journal to record your expenses. By tracking your expenses, you can come up with a plan to save as well as invest your earnings. This will help you make conscious decisions about whether a specific expense is necessary or not. Once you are aware of all your expenses, it becomes easier to get rid of any unnecessary expenses. This is one of the easiest ways to start budgeting.

Spend Less

Did you know that Warren Buffett purchased a house in 1958 $31,500 and has been staying in that house ever since? He is amongst the richest men in society today, and he still stays in the same house. He can obviously afford anything that he wants but showing a little prudence when it comes to expenditure is a good idea. There was a point when Kanye West was neck-deep in debts. Both of these gentlemen were quite rich and famous. However, what is the difference between them? The only difference is that one of them spent money only when he needed to and didn't spend more than he needed. You will be a step closer to financial independence if you cut back on expenses. For instance, let's assume that you spend $2000 on your monthly expenses. Now, instead of spending $ 2000, if you spend only $1500, you can save $500. It might not seem like a significant amount right now, but it will undoubtedly help you save in the long run. When it comes to attaining financial independence, even the smallest of changes you make to your spending habits can be quite significant.

Start Paying yourself

As soon as you get your monthly paycheck, it can be quite tempting to spend it all. However, make sure that you pay yourself first before you spend on anything else. It essentially means that you are required to set a specific amount aside from your paycheck before using it for any other expenses. This is one of the easiest ways to save money. For instance, if you set aside the amount of $500 as soon as you get your salary, you can use the rest for your other expenses. So, at the end of the month, even if you haven't saved anything else, your savings will still be $500. When you start following this tip, you are setting aside funds that you can invest in. Ensure that you receive a fixed amount every month. Spending first and then saving the rest would almost never work, saving first, however, and then living on the rest, yeah, that's a better way to save.

Setting Goals

Now that we have established that money is not the root of all evil, it is time to set goals for you. Why do you want to earn money? What are the needs you wish to fulfill? Do you have any specific goals that you want to attain? Well, the reasons differ from one person to another. For instance, you might want to save up for your retirement or your child's education. You might want to have the financial independence necessary to quit your regular job and do something that you love. Or maybe you need funds to start your own business.

It is time to make a list of all your goals. It is quite motivating when you see yourself making progress toward your goals. Regardless of the pace, you travel at; it does help to know that you are a step closer to your goal than you were before. For instance, if you want to be debt-free, it is quite motivating whenever you pay your debts. As you watch savings increase and your debts diminish, you will feel better. Every step that you take toward your goals will give you the motivation to keep going.

Make a list of your goals and place it so that you can glance at it daily. While setting goals, please make sure that you are setting realistic and attainable goals. Also, make sure that the goals you set are time-bound. If you set a time limit to attain a specific goal, then procrastination will not creep in. It was supposed to end there. The goal of trying to pay off your student loans worth $25,000 in 12 months is an example of an ideal goal. This goal is realistic, attainable, measurable, and time-bound. If the goal you set meets all these criteria, then you are on the right path. If you set unattainable or impractical goals for yourself, you are setting yourself up for disappointment. If you know what you need to attain, it becomes easier to take steps to achieve that goal.

Start Paying Off Your Debts

You will be a step closer to financial independence if you are debt-free. Now that you are aware of all your debts, start clearing them one after the other. Clearing your debts can give you the motivation and the confidence to attain financial independence. If you want, you can start with the smallest debt and slowly make your way to the major ones. Or you can also start with any significant liability you have like a mortgage or a student loan and clear that first. If you have a couple of debts, then make a list of those debts according to the interest payable. Start by clearing off those debts with the highest interest rate. For instance, if you have two loans repayable at 17% and 6% of interest, then repay the one with the 17% interest first. If you are paying a high rate of interest on any loans, then it will take you longer to repay the principal. Instead of wasting your money by paying unnecessary interest, it is better to repay that loan. Also, whenever you clear off a debt, you will undoubtedly feel quite relieved.

Additional Streams of Income

A lot of people often wonder how they can ever pay their debts and attain financial freedom when they don't have sufficient income. If you want financial independence, then remember that it will take a conscious effort, dedication, and time. This isn't something that you can achieve overnight. If you realize that your regular job isn't sufficient to help you attain this goal, then it is time to consider additional streams of income. You can earn money through active work as well as other passive sources of revenue. Any activity that you undertake, which requires your active involvement is referred to as active income. For instance, your regular job or even trading is an active income. Any income that you obtain with minimum effort is passive income. If you have a passion for writing and are good at it, then you can become a freelance writer. You can pick up the job of a virtual assistant or become an Uber driver if you want. There are different streams of income available to you provided you look for them. You don't have to restrict yourself to your regular job. Start looking for additional sources of revenue.

To do this, start by making a list of all the things that you're good at and the skills you possess. Apart from this, consider your daily schedule and analyze the time which you can devote your additional streams. For instance, you can start a drop shipping business, become an affiliate marketer, or even use Amazon FBA to create passive income. Apart from this, you can also generate income from any rental property you own. There are different avenues available, so start looking for them today. A great way to supplement your regular income is via investing. You will learn more about investments in the subsequent parts.

Chapter 7:

Be Successful in Business

Let's face a harsh reality. Howsoever hard you try to build a new self-image by setting new beliefs, if the people or environment around are not supportive, you will face a really tough time.

You know that climbing a mountain requires lots of effort, dedication, the application of strategies and persistence. More than physical, it requires mental toughness. But falling from the mountain doesn't take any effort. Merely by letting yourself drop the ropes, you will be instantly pulled by the force of gravity towards a deep valley.

Similarly, on the personal growth journey, there will be people around you who will not support you; rather, they might make fun of or ridicule you for your efforts in developing new habits or behaviors. Your endeavor to improve yourself is like climbing a mountain: it takes time. But getting affected by unsupportive people and a negative environment is like falling down, and it happens instantly if you don't safeguard yourself.

Therefore, you need to be careful with such people and any kind of environment that distracts you or pulls you away from the path of a growth mindset.

You now know that backed by neuroscience, the concept of neuroplasticity works on the principle of changing your environment and behavior, you can change your mind. To put it bluntly, your mindset can never exceed the mindset of people you generally hang out with.

Therefore, you need to design your environment to the best possible extent. The environment designing process is done in two ways-

- You need to protect yourself from a negative environment and simultaneously
- You need to structure your day and take the time to infuse more positivity into your life

Let's start with how to deal with a negative environment created by the people around us.

Set Goals

The most important requirements to be successful:

Smart

It is Specific, Measurable, Attainable, Realistic and Timely. I, in general, subscribe to this thinking though I think the "A" and "R" can be up for some debate. Your goals need to be specific because if they are a vague statement such as "sell a lot of real estates" how will you ever know if you achieve it? Is that $1 million in sales? $5 million? $50 million? If you aren't specific, you will never know what you are striving for, how much more you have to go to attain, etc.

Measurable is the next one. Obviously, you need to be able to assess how you are doing with a goal, so having measurable goals is needed. Setting a goal to sell $1 million/month is measurable because at the end of the month, you can add up your sales and see if it gets to $1 million.

Attainable and Realistic are the two that some may have questions about. Some experts will say "Reach for the moon and even if you fail, you can still hit a star." These items are subjective, and you can decide what realistic and attainable mean to you. My recommendation is always to push yourself just one step further than you are comfortable. If you think $2 million in sales is a realistic and attainable goal, set it at $2.2 or $2.4 million. I have often found when you stretch your goals, you stretch your brain. Setting your sights, a little higher force you to think more outside the box and creatively find ways to achieve results never before achieved.

Lastly, timing is key. You can have a specific, measurable and realistic goal, but if you don't put a due date it's not overly useful. Setting a time limit is essential. Do you want to achieve that goal in a month or a year? How about setting goals for the day? It's all up to you but giving yourself that due date helps you focus and motivate yourself.

So, time to take a break from reading and learning. It's time to implement one of our first lessons of "Just Do

It." Do you have goals you have written down for this year? If so, congratulations.

There is no one magic formula for success. Success requires multiple behaviors you must implement in your life; it requires a different mindset but most importantly it requires the following attitude.

Desire

Why do people become successful?

Because they desire something, whether it is a dream car, traveling the world, being able to give to people, or just freedom, successful people desire a change in their life.

All desire is, is change. When you desire something badly enough you will do absolutely anything in your power to get it. You become so obsessed with this thing you desire that nothing can come in the way of you and your desire.

Most people want more money in their life, but they don't desire more money in their life. Most people want happiness, but they don't do anything to fulfill that happiness. If they desired happiness, they would do what makes them happy.

When you see people succeed, it is because of a deep desire they have. If you don't truly desire to become successful, then you will give up once you encounter your first failure. When someone will tell you to give up you would because you don't truly desire success.

If there is something in your life right now, it is because you desired it. Whether it's the perfect husband or wife or your car or your job or even a physical transformation, you have it in your life because of your desire towards it.

The difference between want and desire is what you are doing today to achieve what you want. People want to be healthy but very few people are willing to change their diet or exercise. If you truly desire to become healthy you will wake up early to have more time to work out. Same with getting a six-pack. Many people wish they had a six-pack but only people who truly desire one will work hard enough to get it.

It's simple; with no desire you are guaranteed to fail.

The law of attraction states that you must visualize what you want to manifest. Visualizing is the best way to create more desire. You can wish to have a Lamborghini and that might give you enough motivation to work for an hour.

You can visualize sitting on the racing seats in a Lamborghini. You can visualize the steering wheel staring you in the face. You can imagine how it would feel to grip your hands on the steering wheel. You can hear the engine roar as you start up the car. You can visualize yourself driving the Lamborghini at dangerous speeds. That will keep you motivated for the whole day.

Visualizing amplifies your desire, which amplifies your work ethic.

Your brain is designed to solve problems. That is the sole purpose of having a brain. If you're hungry, your brain will find a way to get food. Just like if you want to be successful, your brain will find a way to make you successful, but you must become obsessed with success.

When your problem isn't important enough to you, your brain will ignore it. When you are at a point where you want to change, and you become obsessed with that change, your brain will find a solution to your problem.

If you want to make money and you truly want it and become obsessed with it, your brain will try and fix your problem. When you become obsessed with making money your brain will give you so many opportunities to help you make money. It will open up doors for you; you didn't even know were there. The only thing you need to do is take advantage of these opportunities.

Studies show that 53% of self-made millionaires were obsessed with becoming rich and successful before they were wealthy.

Clarity

It is very important to be clear when it comes to setting goals. You can't just say "I want to be successful" or "I want to be a millionaire." You need to get clear on exactly want you want.

When you set goals, you need to write down these 3 specific elements.

1. Exactly what you want
2. The exact date you want to achieve your goal
3. Exactly how you are going to achieve that goal

For example, your goal can be to make some money. You must include all three of the points mentioned above so you can have a clear goal.

"I want to make $5,000 by the 1st of July. I will achieve this goal by making 3 YouTube videos a week and monetizing them."

When you get specific your goal seems so much simpler. When you are clear then that means you are certain. You have a plan now all that's left to execute.

If you haven't already, I want you to stop reading this guidebook and write down some clear goals. Make sure to include what your goal is (it might be buying a car or a house, it might be to finish a drawing or write a book) then write down the exact date you want it done by and exactly how you are going to achieve that goal.

If your goal is to write a book your goal should look like this: "I want to write a book on the millionaire money mind-set, and have it finished by 23rd of September. I will do this by writing down my knowledge and then organizing it into a layout. Then I will write a page a day until my book is completed and published on Amazon."

Since you will see your goal written down it will motivate you to achieve it and it is more likely to stick. Your brain will also see that you have a problem and it will try its best to fix it.

Chapter 8:

Change Lifestyle

Keep Up in Change

How many times have you heard change is the only constant? It's a cliché, but it's true. Thirty years ago, well before the Internet, Google, and social media, Alvin Toffler wrote about the accelerating pace of change in his groundbreaking book, Future Shock. Today, future shock is leading to the creative disruption of industries and lifestyles. The rapid absorption of rapidly evolving technology is destroying old industries and creating new ones almost overnight:

- Cloud computing and tablet technology are marginalizing PCs
- Smartphones have pretty much replaced digital point-and-shoot cameras which replaced film cameras

- Streaming replaced CDs which replaced cassettes which replaced vinyl records

Texting is an upstaging email that replaced faxes which replaced snail mail.

More importantly, the availability of relatively inexpensive and easy-to-use consumer technology has linked people throughout the world to create a global marketplace of ideas, information, and services. Of course, everyone is aware of offshore manufacturing and call centers, but did you know:

American corporations hire out a lot of their accounting and legal work to lower-cost overseas providers?

American news organizations hire services in India that scan American public records and police reports writing local news?

You can hire a web developer in Karachi, Pakistan, who charges less and may do a better job than one living down the block?

While the forces of globalization have lifted over 600 million people out of poverty worldwide — about double the population of the U.S. — the American middle class feels squeezed. In spite of a low unemployment rate, a huge percentage of the American workforce is underemployed and underpaid. According to Gallup, only 45% of American workers have good jobs. Good jobs, as defined by Gallup, are positions that offer at least thirty hours/week from employers that provide regular paychecks. By this definition, many minimum-wage service jobs, which often don't pay enough to live on, are considered "good."

The question is, will growing demand from the world's expanding middle class create more and better job opportunities for Americans, or will increasing automation and global competition continue to keep wages down? As we grapple with the changing realities of the new global economy, some things are clear:

Corporations will continue to hire more part-time and contract workers so they can quickly expand and contract their workforces to meet changing demand for products and services. With more temporary employees, they also avoid high benefit costs.

Well-paying jobs require an educated workforce. The opportunity and income gap between those with and without education will continue to grow.

Given the pace of technological change, new industries and jobs will come and go with increasing speed. To remain relevant, workers will have to keep their knowledge and skills current through continuing education.

One big uncertainty is the cost of higher education. Will young people from lower and middle-income households be able to afford the education and training they need to compete in the global economy effectively? Another uncertainty is the future of Medicare and Social Security. According to the latest projections, they'll remain solvent until about 2030, when they'll no longer have enough money to fund all their obligations. By the time millennia's reach retirement age, these programs may not exist in their current form: benefits could be reduced, retirement age could be extended, means testing could determine eligibility, or they could be completely reimagined.

The good news, if you're a millennial, is that time is on your side. Other than health, time is your most valuable asset. Following the guidelines in this guidebook, be sure to use it wisely:

- Acquire the education and/or training you to need to earn a decent living
- Keep your knowledge and skills up to date
- Engage in meaningful social interactions
- Give to others
- Anticipate and plan for the future
- Invest your savings early and often
- Give your investments time to grow.

Stay Prepared

Keeping your skills current is one of the best ways to assure financial success because you need to make money before you can save and invest it. Whether you pursue vocational training or a university degree, it helps to be both a specialist and generalist to succeed in today's workplace. If you don't specialize, you may not get the job:

- You need a medical degree to treat patients at the hospital
- You need a dental hygienist certificate to clean teeth
- You need mechatronics training to operate automated manufacturing equipment

If an employer is looking for a programmer with JavaScript experience, she may not care that you're a Pascal expert.

With so much competition in the job market today, you may not get the interview if your skills don't perfectly match the employer's needs. But specialists run the risk of obsolescence. I'm guessing that about 60% of jobs today didn't exist thirty years ago, at least not in their current form. Thirty years ago, there were no app developers, social media specialists, genomic therapists, or Body Pump instructors. If you're a BASIC programmer, printer, stenographer, or even secretary, finding a job today could be tough.

While focusing on your specialty, protect your employability by developing generalist traits. Expand your horizons by pursuing your interests in music, philosophy, environmentalism, or extreme sports, even when they do not pay. Consider volunteering your time to support a cause you believe in. Conduct a church choir. Coach a little league team.

When you stretch your muscles by exercising new skills, you develop the resilience and adaptive capacity to respond to changes in the workplace. When the job grows, so can you. When your company announces that it will be switching from circuit board production to farming hydroponic lettuce — yes, you read this correctly1 — your heart may skip a beat or two, but you won't be thrown completely off balance. If your company contracts or folds, you'll be able to adapt and transfer your experience and skills from one job to another with greater ease than someone who is overly specialized.

A Word on Aging

Though we wrote the $500 Cup of Coffee mostly for young people, I can't resist the temptation to include a few words on aging. After all, this guidebook focuses on planning a financially secure future.

Today's notions of age and aging are different from when Dave and I grew up. When we were young, thirty was over the hill. Today thirty is young and sixty is the new forty. Thanks to healthier lifestyle choices and advances in medical care, people are living longer, more active lives.

While baby boomers tend to look back at our youth with fondness, the transition years from student to working adult were some of the most challenging times of life. With friends, jobs, and living arrangements all in flux, we didn't know where or how we'd land. Decision-making was fraught with anxiety because it seemed like every choice had the potential to set or upset our life course. What if we chose the wrong school, major, boyfriend, girlfriend, or job?

But, as we learned, things have a way of working out. In spite of all the handwringing and soul-searching, most of us survived our youthful indiscretions and learned from our mistakes. We eventually settled on career, home, and family, though life remained pretty hectic, especially for those who raised a family while working. Yes, we lost sleep and control of our time, but the rewards—starting with hugs, kisses, and laughter—made it worthwhile.

Despite the rewards, life, at times, can feel like a steady parade of challenges. Confronted by job loss, divorce, or the care of an elderly relative, some people crumble under the pressure, but most taps into hidden reserves of strength that they didn't know were there. Although they may meltdown in the heat of the moment, like steel tempered by fire, they often emerge from crises stronger, more self-aware, and confident.

This confidence extends from the boardroom to the bedroom. While you may think that physical intimacy is for the young and beautiful, many people find mature sex more satisfying and enjoyable. Midlife women are more comfortable in their skin than twenty and thirty-something's and have the confidence, experience, and desire to be more daring in bed. Likewise, middle-aged men feel less pressure to perform. Yes, aging can be freeing:

- As we further mature, we experience greater self-acceptance and tend to care less about what others think and say

- We no longer feel pressure to prove ourselves because we've already accomplished so much
- We know from experience that we have the coping skills to make it through the next set of challenges, so we worry less
- We take ourselves less seriously and react less personally to events beyond our control

Even when things are not exactly as we'd like, we're more likely to accept them as they are.

In older age, we spend less time fighting the things we cannot change and more time enjoying the fruits of our labor. Rather than something to fear, older age can be a wonderful time of life, especially for those with good health and financial security.

Chapter 9:

Train Your Memory

Continuous Learning

To grow yourself as an individual and become more focused, you need to learn how to ask the right questions and actively listen to people. Train yourself to become a good listener: one who listens carefully before responding rather than trying to dominate every conversion.

No one knows everything. No one includes you.

Successful people never stop learning. Even when they "make it," they continue to learn and absorb new information.

Today, reading seems like an uncool thing to do. Schools have made reading seem like a punishment instead of something you do to improve yourself and to grow. If you don't read, then you can't grow as a person.

I think the reason most people don't read isn't that they don't like reading, but it's because they don't believe that a small $10 book can hold information that can truly change their lives.

Everyone thinks that they are the smartest person on earth. They think that they know everything, and they can't learn anything new. They see a book on how to become healthy and they think "I don't need a book to tell me how to be healthy all you have to do is exercise and eat the right foods."

Successful people understand the power of books. You can open a book and learn the entire life story of someone. Some people have autobiographies made about them. 80 years of knowledge, experiences, stories, and lessons all packed into a small 300-page book.

Most people think education stops the moment you finish high school or university or college. It doesn't. Every successful person knows that education never stops.

Whether you are buying books or courses or are paying for seminars you should always keep learning. You never know what information you might learn. You could pay $500 for a course and only learn one new thing, but that new thing might take your business to the level. The level that will make you an extra $2000 a month.

People don't read books because it's easier not to. It's more enjoyable to watch an entertaining video rather than read a book. People value entertainment more than knowledge which is why most people aren't successful.

If you scroll through your YouTube history list, keep going down and count how many entertaining videos you watched before you watched an educational video. A video that will help you grow or will give you some value.

Read books that will help you grow your business or have better relationships with your friends or help you make money or help you lose weight. Read something that will impact your life.

Successful people don't read "The Hobbit" or "Harry Potter." They read books that will make an impact on them. They read biographies of successful people and see how they solved their problems or overcame their failures. Read for knowledge not for entertainment.

It's not enough to just read. The more books you read, the more knowledge you will have but it's what you do with that knowledge that matters. If you just read, then all you have is knowledge. You need to find a way to turn that knowledge into something meaningful.

Become Valuable

The mistake that most people make is they chase money. They try to find a solution to make money. The thing is you don't make money; money needs to come to you. Money is attracted to value.

People aren't paid based on how long they work; they are paid by the value they bring to the time. That's why someone who works at McDonald's will get a minimum wage while graphic designers and programmers get paid 30 dollars an hour. Anyone can become a McDonald's employee which doesn't make them valuable to the marketplace. Becoming a programmer though is time-consuming and is a skill not many people pursue; programmers are more valuable in the marketplace which makes them worth more money.

It is simple if you want to create wealth, you must first become valuable enough for that wealth. Value takes time.

There was once a locksmith who would unlock the people's lock in his neighborhood. One day a man asked the locksmith to unlock his door because he forgot his keys. The locksmith grabbed his tools and started picking the lock. 2 hours later he finally unlocked the lock and charged the man $250.

The next day a woman approaches the locksmith and asks him to unlock her door because she forgot her keys. Again, he brought his tools and started picking the lock. He managed to unlock the door within an hour. He then charged her $250.

After a few months, he had unlocked so many locks he was able to unlock it within 10 minutes. A man asked the locksmith to unlock his door because he forgot his keys. The locksmith took his toolbox out and started picking the lock. 10 minutes later he unlocked the door. He charged the man $250.

"I'm not paying $250," said the man / "Why not? I unlocked the door," said the locksmith.

"That took 10 minutes. I have to work 25 hours to earn $250 not 10 minutes," said the man.

What the man doesn't realize was the locksmith wasn't charging by his time he was charging based on the value he brought. Ove time, he became more valuable because he was able to unlock the door within minutes.

The man doesn't realize that the locksmith had experience under his belt. He doesn't know that it used to take him 2 hours to pick his lock. The locksmith should have charged more since he did the job faster than anyone else.

Become the best and you can achieve success. If you become valuable in your market money will follow. If you are the greatest motivational speaker in the world, people will pay you a lot of money for your services.

People are paid on the value they provide not by the amount of time they work or how hard they worked.

Care what you Wish for

But how should we feel or think to optimize our results? Is there any attitude we can adopt that boosts the qualities of our work?

Your mindset plays a huge factor when it comes down to the quality of your work. You should connect with it, put in your soul and come from a place of caring. When you care, you put yourself in an optimal state to produce the highest quality you're currently capable of. It primes your mind to take it seriously, because you're producing something that is part of who you are. However, at the moment your care-level drops, you will start to slack, bungle and become distracted or impatient. Why? Because you hold yourself back from doing better. Subconsciously, you know you're not giving it your best. Thereby, your creation will suffer, and this starts to eat at your consciousness. A half-assed creation will provide false evidence for your lack of skill. This can induce fear, like doubts, incompetency and insecurity. After all, you just proved yourself not to be good enough and your work confirms that.

So, by lowering the bar of what you're truly capable of, you can hurt yourself as well as others. You see, if your half-assed creation is to be shared with others, you will not treat them optimally. After all, you have the qualities to give them something better. This is taking the easy way out and it will show. People will notice the lack of quality and pick up that you try to get off easy. In response, they may not appreciate it or feel that it's a waste of time. Just ask yourself; what do you think what would happen when we all treat each other without caring? Alternatively, what do you think would happen when we all treat each other with full care? What do you think is a more optimal way of living?

Whether we like to admit it or not, our work will always reflect how much we care. The amount of care shows the truth of our love-based and fear-based motives. If we come from a place of love for our work, the results will reflect this higher quality. If we come from a place of fear, our endeavors will automatically show this lower quality, especially in the long run. Thereby, anything fruitful and sustainable originates from love-based motives. Anything unfruitful and unsustainable originates from fear-based motives.

That's why, all it takes is a positive mindset to get on the right path. The path is already there. You just have to choose to walk it.

Manage your Risk

Risk is unavoidable. No matter how careful you are, every time you leave home, you run the risk of being hit by a car. Sometimes you don't even have to leave the house. How many times have you heard about cars plowing through bedroom walls pinning people to their beds?

While accidents will happen, you can manage most risks through education and planning. Premarital counseling, for example, can reduce the risk of divorce by helping couples set realistic expectations for married life, which is more about working together and compromise than sunsets and romance. Starting a new business is also risky, but you can mitigate the risk by preparing a realistic business plan and cash flow analysis. Likewise, you can manage your investment risk by carefully researching different investment vehicles and opportunities and/or consulting a financial advisor. If you have never invested, or even if you have, it's always a good idea to consult an expert who works full-time understanding the financial markets.

A good financial advisor will help you look at and understand your tolerance for risk. If you lose sleep every time the market falls, you probably shouldn't invest in stocks. If you are overwhelmed by the expense and/or the responsibilities of homeownership, buying a home may not be a good option for you. While a good financial advisor will not recommend investments that will cost you sleep at night or tie your stomach in knots, she will encourage reasonable risk, so that your investment dollars can grow. On the other hand, if you have a cast-iron belly and you're willing to bet the entire farm on a single high-risk opportunity, she'll encourage you to curb your enthusiasm and diversify your investments, so if your surefire bet goes bust, you'll still have enough left to feed the chickens.

Obviously, too much risk is foolhardy, but so is too much caution. Do you really want to spend the rest of your life paying off your landlord's mortgage while your savings are earning close to zero percent interest?

Striking the right balance is key. When you're young, you can afford to take more chances even if you're cautious by nature. You have plenty of time to recover from any losses, while the power of compound interest continues to grow your investments over the next three, four, or even five decades. If you are older and looking at a shorter investment horizon, you may not have time to recover from a big hit, so more caution is advised.

As you transition from your twenties to thirties to forties and so on, your circumstances, personal goals, and risk tolerance change. Fortunately, you can adjust your investment strategy and rebalance your asset portfolio to keep pace with your changing needs.

Chapter 10:

Never Give Up

Patience Is a Virtue

Never give up. Patience is a virtue. Most successful people today are people who never believed in failure. Rather, they take failure as a learning curve to grow. They had worked smart to be where they are today. It takes hope, focus, and sheer determination to achieve success.

Learn from Your Failures

If you want to succeed in anything you do, then you have to learn from your failures and use what you've learned to progress forward. It's this simple - GET OVER IT! Nearly half of businesses fail within three years. But the only entrepreneurs that really fail are the ones who don't get back up and try again. Everyone else learns from their failings and uses it to find a successful business model.

If you're ready to succeed, then you should follow these simple tips:

I. Understand what it takes to be successful at whatever you want to accomplish before beginning.
II. Determine your strengths and weaknesses. Get an outside perspective and have them tell you whether you're as competent as you think you are in your chosen field.
III. Continue to build your strengths if you aren't yet ready for the responsibility of your dreams or goals if you need to. Or bring in other people to assist you with their expertise so that you can accomplish your goal together.
IV. Plan ahead to be successful. Know what your expectations are for the month. What do you want to achieve? How did your previous month differ? Then use that information to make a plan to succeed.

Businesses Carry Hefty Risks

Different businesses carry different risks. Your ability to envision how to provide a solution to other people through the business puts you at the forefront of withstanding any eventualities.

All businesses have one thing in common - Accounts Balance: Balance Sheet/Profit & Loss Account; Revenue (Money in); Expenditure (Money out); Assets, and Liabilities.

Having a good understanding of how money functions would help you avoid making risky business decisions. Because many people had failed in their businesses does not mean that you too would be scared to chase your own dreams.

Life itself is a risk. Our existence today carries its own risk, but it is our inability to spot those risks and avert them that put us in more danger than the risk itself.

Come Up with a Business Idea

Thinking about a new business idea is quite tricky because you would not even know if that business would be the right business for you at this time of the year. Whatever happens, you will have to come up with the best business idea you can ever conceive. Always remember to avoid businesses with high operating costs, except if you are sure you will secure some external investments.

Brainstorm some business ideas, and perhaps meet with your business partner/s to discuss them. Make a list of all business ideas you have in mind, and eliminate each, one after another until you reach the final idea you are passionate about. And a business you know you cannot do without.

I remembered that between 2009 and 2011 before I went solo, I had contacted some close friends, and former classmates to discuss the potential for collaboration, and starting a Pharmacy business in Manchester. All of them turned the opportunity down. I remembered that one of the reasons I was given was that starting a Pharmacy business was quite risky.

Yeah, they were right. Business is risky, just like life itself. Not everyone was born an entrepreneur and risk-takers. If you are reading this guidebook, and hoping to start a new business with your friends or family members as business partners, one thing I can assure you is that you have to be ready to accept rejection by those closest to you and those whom you call your friends. Out of envy or jealousy, your friends may keep their distance from you when your business starts booming. Do not worry. It's time to move on. Keep busy and continue to make a difference in the world through your business.

What kept me going was the fact that not everyone was born to take risks. My advice is always never to give up. Every problem has a solution. We were created by God in His own image, and in His own likeness (Genesis 1: 26-27). Every bad situation should not be called a 'problem', rather an opportunity to reflect on what went wrong in the past, and what next steps to follow to resolve the problem in the future.

God who created you and gave you dominion over all things created by Him shall give you the knowledge, and the wisdom to conquer the world, which is your gifting, your career, or profession. For in Him all things were created: things in heaven and on earth (Colossians 1:16).

Challenge yourself

It's really easy to avoid doing the things that we want in life because of the risk that's involved in being happy. That's right... you'd rather be miserable in life with a career that you don't like than do what makes you happy. Why do you ask? Because it's so comfortable to conform to the status quo. There's a solution to this, however. It's called taking a risk.

First off, if you've considered taking a risk and have decided against it then you're not alone. Most people focus only on what can go wrong and limit themselves before ever getting close to success. The funny thing is that people usually overestimate the probability that something will go wrong while ignoring the potential benefits by magnifying our imaginations.

So instead of acting, most people just stick to normal everyday activities. But think about this, what are you giving up by being inactive? Things aren't going to change in your life unless you do it dramatically. When you play it safe, you stay at the same point that you've always been in while the issues in your life grow larger.

So how do you learn how to take risks?

- Plan out your method of action.
- Have faith that you'll succeed.

- Execute your plan.

- Evaluate your performance.

- Think about the next goal and repeat it.

It's simple, isn't it? Start looking at the positives and weighing it just as much as the negatives, and you'll begin to find the benefit in going after your goals and dreams instead of waiting for them to come to you.

Run a Strong Marketing Campaign

With the growth of the internet and most of your potential customers hooked online, it is no wonder online marketing campaigns are one of the best ways to let your customers know that you have arrived. I remembered a night before the launch of my business, I went crazy with online marketing through Google and Facebook. With Facebook, I was able to post messages and gathered "followers" using friends and family members across the world. Within a week of launching our business campaign, people started calling, and the phone was buzzing with calls and inquiries. With annual Public Health campaigns, it was an opportunity to tell the world what we offer, and how we can add value to make their lives better compared to our competitors.

As our businesses grew day-by-day, and months into years, we continued the execution of paid advertising using Door-2-Door Leaflet Distribution Companies in Manchester such as RCD, Google, GP surgery appointment cards, Yell.com or the HibuGroup.com - the publishers of Yellow Pages – one of the UK's leading online business directories. We believe that over 60,000 leaflets were distributed including our own distributions in Churches, Mosques, Schools, Playgrounds, etc.

Our marketing campaigns took us across full pages of local Newspapers, Church Magazines, as well as in the front and back pages of the Bleckley & Muston Life Magazine – a monthly business magazine published by a local in Middleton Greater Manchester which targeted most sought after homes in Bleckley and Muston areas of Manchester.

Be Ready to Work Long Hours

There is always the temptation that as the owner of a new business, that you can "pick and choose" when you want to work and where you want to be. Sometimes, this may not be so especially in the early years of starting your new business. It is like having a new-born baby. Your new business needs your attention to growing. If you leave your business to be managed by employees in the earlier stages, it is likely bound to fail, or it may not pick up the way you had planned it to be. Most business owners are known to work long hours up to 20 hours a day, including weekends.

No matter how lucrative your main job is, your new business still needs your attention to driving business strategies. Be ready to put in many hours in the first year and continue to show your presence in the months to come.

By having the first-hand knowledge of what goes on in the new business, you would get to know your customers, establish business relations, and devise strategies to meet their needs. Focus on Growth.

Whatever growth means to you, you are in business to make profits, and grow. While the essence of your business is to solve problems in a niche market, focusing on growth allows you to reach as many customers as possible - nationally, and globally. Continuously inventing and reinventing you again and again, and consistently finding ways to increase your business efficiency with lower costs are some of the many ways to grow.

Work Smart

Your quest to creating a profitable business and a million-pound GBP turnover does not mean that you must work too hard. Working hard means putting too many hours to complete a project, while working smart means working fewer hours to achieve the same project outcomes. As a business owner, you will prioritize which important board meetings to attend, best employees and professionals to recruit, and the best friends to meet and focus on driving the business strategies forward.

Chapter 11:

Self-Discipline

Self-discipline is the ability of a person to control their impulses, reactions, behaviors, and emotions. It allows them to let go of instant gratification in exchange for long-term gain and satisfaction. It's the act of saying no when you really want to say yes. Self-discipline isn't about living a restrictive and boring life without any enjoyment. In fact, it's almost impossible to be 100% self-disciplined in every single area of your life. Interspersed throughout this guidebook are various recommendations for saving you at the last moment when you feel like you don't have any discipline left. This specific part highlights additional valuable techniques.

Create a Solid Plan

When you notice your willpower starting to get depleted, you can always go back to the plan you have developed, as well as the goal you have set so that you can mitigate the negative effects of lowered willpower. While it's true that even those who have developed the most solid plans are still at risk of failing (since there's actually no guarantee that you will be successful all the time), having it around will help keep you move forward despite challenges. This means that you'll continue trying until you see all the steps in your plan taken into action.

Eat and Hydrate Well

You have to eat well to prevent your self-discipline and willpower from depleting. Note that nutrition is extremely useful in the proper functioning of your brain. The brain cells that are working to retain a high level of self-control also require sugar or glucose. If you have low glucose, then there is a risk for your brain to respond strongly to instant rewards. This causes you to disregard your long-term goal.

Fortunately, it is easy to maintain a healthy level of glucose in your body. All it takes is to consume balanced meals with the right amount of fiber and protein. It can also raise your energy and keep you mentally alert, thereby preventing you from succumbing to potential temptations and making impulsive decisions.

Hydration is also essential to overall nutrition. Note that a lack of water can hamper your cognitive performance. Water is crucial whether you are in your class, in the workplace or at the gym. You need around 1-4 liters of water daily to ensure that your mind functions well.

There are also times when people confuse thirst with hunger. In case you feel hungry even if it's not yet your mealtime, consider reaching for one glass of water instead of a snack. You have a lower risk of losing your willpower and self-discipline by letting your brain and body function at their best. That's possible through a healthy and balanced diet and proper hydration.

Get enough Sleep

Getting enough sleep is essential in allowing your brain to manage your energy more efficiently. It also plays a huge rule in ensuring that your prefrontal cortex works at its best. Depriving yourself of sleep, which usually happens when you just get less than six hours of sleep per night, can cause you to experience chronic stress, which tends to damage the way your brain and body utilize energy. Your prefrontal cortex suffers the blow the most, causing some parts of your brain, especially those that form cravings and stress response to lose control.

You can prevent this from happening by ensuring that you get high quality and enough sleep each night. Go for 7-8 hours of sleep every night. Sleep researchers prove that those who get enough hours of sleep actually live happier and longer. They are also more productive. This is the main reason why even the best athletes, who need to have the highest level of self-control and discipline, have their own sleep couches. This helps ensure that they still get their needed amount of sleep despite all the training that they need to do.

Adequate and quality sleep can also prevent you from dealing with excessive tiredness that may only impair your awareness, reaction time and damage. It should also be noted that lack of sleep can change hormones that regulate appetite in your body. This can also impair your metabolism. That said, it's time to make it a habit to have enough sleep each night.

Improve the Flexibility of your Mind

Having a more resilient and flexible mind is crucial in boosting willpower. You can improve your mind's flexibility and resiliency by embracing changes and accepting challenges. With this improvement, it will be easier for your brain to form constructive responses to stressful circumstances. Your goal should be to direct your mind to what you want to achieve especially for the long term, instead of letting past failures and setbacks control you.

Make the Most Out of your Imagination

Using your imagination is one of the most powerful techniques in boosting your discipline and willpower. Note that your body has the tendency to respond well to situations that you've imagined similar to the situations you actually experienced. For instance, imagine that you are currently in a peaceful beach that allows your body to respond by relaxing. Imagining that you arrived at a meeting with your presentation unprepared may also cause your body to tense up. Your body's reaction to your imagination is useful in improving your willpower.

When implementing the tips mentioned in this part, keep in mind that no matter how smart and talented you are, you will still have a hard time reaching for your goals if you don't have self-discipline and willpower. You need to develop self-control as it helps you in balancing your immediate wants and needs and your long-term goals.

While cultivating discipline and developing strong willpower is not that easy (you can't expect it to happen with just one meditation or relaxation session), note that performing certain practices on a regular basis is helpful for you. Just like other things in life, trying to establish more meaningful and purposeful habits requires a lot of commitment on your part. With strong willpower and discipline, it will be easier for you to stick to your goals.

Focus — the Secret Weapon

Focus is powerful. The rays of the sun do not burn anything unless and until you bring them into focus. The fact that you're reading this right now says you understand the importance of focus when it comes to matters of discipline.

Focus is all about being able to pay very close attention to anyone thing or subject for a long period of time. You could think of this fun little acronym when you think of focus: Follow One Course

Until-Success

Now, let's take a quick look at why it matters so much that you learn to build your focus in your day to day life.

1. Focus is a stress and anxiety buster. Take a moment and consider any aspect of your life right now, whether it's your finances, family, home, work, or whatever matters to you, really. If you cannot pay that area of your life the needed attention, it will inevitably begin to suffer. If you make a habit of getting distracted by things that don't matter, then you're going to be in a world of hurt.

   If you don't do the work you're supposed to, you're only letting the inevitable pile up, until you feel paralyzed by anxiety and overwhelmed over it all, so you've got to sleep less and take your work home with you. If you're in college, or you're taking some course, when you don't focus, you're going to give yourself way too much to assimilate in way too little time.

   A lack of focus inevitably will lead to you feeling stressed, frustrated, and overwhelmed. This is why you've got to build your focus, as it lets you concentrate wholly on the task at hand and keeps you from creating stressful situations for yourself.

2. Focus works wonders for your creativity. It has been observed that when you're not really paying attention to anything specific, creative ideas come to you. That is not what I'm talking about right now, though. This sort of idleness is valid, even according to neuroscience, as it gives your mind the room to come up with fantastic ideas. What I'm talking about now, though, is the creativity that comes when you have decided to work on the best idea that has occurred to you.

When you've figured out what you need to work on, then you've got to make it happen. You've got to give that idea some flesh on its bones, and then put it out there so that it's real. Let's assume that you've got to start up a new project, or you need to resume something you started the day before. The first 10 to 15 minutes are the hardest. However, once you've remained focused for that long, your mind enters the flow state.

The flow state is the same thing as being in the zone. It's when you're totally immersed in what you're doing. You have energy, clarity, and you enjoy what you're doing. This creative zone that you get into is not the reserve of artists. You can experience this no matter what you're creating, whether it's a sculpture or an email.

The brain is designed in such a way that when you focus on something for a long enough period, your neural pathways will begin to work in tandem, doing their best to link all the dots, and get all the information that is relevant to whatever you're doing. If you're facing a problem and you need the solution, the way to find it is through focus.

3. Focus fuels fulfillment. When you are completely focused on what you're doing, you know for a fact that you will deliver quality, and you will meet or even beat the deadlines you have. When you are focused, time no longer exists for you, especially as you are in the flow state.

Have you ever been so immersed in your work that you don't even notice that day has become night? Well, this is the way focus works. Even if it's a couple of lovebirds sitting on a park bench looking at each other in the eye, the same principle applies: Time flies when you're having fun — and focus can bring that fun and fulfillment you need in whatever you do.

As you work with focus, you remain grounded in the present moment. You're not burdening your mind with useless, unneeded thoughts. You feel more fulfilled with the work you're doing because you're grounded in the here and now. You're the happiest ever when you focus on the task at hand, in the present.

4. Focus builds confidence. When you need to deal with a huge task, it can seem scary and overwhelming. You're tempted to procrastinate. The way to beat that is to focus. When you bring in focus, you instinctively split the work into smaller chunks. This way, you can get the ball rolling, and with small, consistent bites, you will eventually finish eating that elephant.

Chapter 12:

Meet People of your Same Level

1. Connect with people who inspire you. It's worth taking the tie to find and meet these people who have done the same thing you're trying to do. When you listen to their story, you will find yourself feeling invigorated, and you will go after your goals with twice as much focus and determination.
2. Take part in group activities. The best way to really connect with your goals is to become a part of group activities that revolve around what you intend to achieve. Say you want to buy a house in a certain suburb; you could drive around and check out the available open houses. If you want to become a trader, you could hang out at trader seminars or conventions, so you can get a feel for what it's like to be a successful trader.

3. Read as many inspirational stories as you can. When you read these stories, you feel a stirring within you that helps you go after what matters the most to you. You get to walk in the shoes of other successful people who have conquered the challenges you gave. You learn what they learn, and you have the cheat codes to get there twice as fast or at least with fewer tears shed along the way.
4. Do something. When you take action, you make progress. That feeling of progress makes you want to keep going. Each action you take brings you that much closer to your goals. So, ask yourself each day what it is you will do that will advance you towards your goal.

The Importance of Having the Right Peer Group and Friends who are Like-Minded

Achieving mastery requires that you set up the right environment to allow yourself to thrive. The truth is that your environment dictates your tastes and influences your decisions in life. By 'environment,' I mean the people you surround yourself with.

You may or not be aware of this when it happens, but the people you hang out with the most are going to rub off on you. You will find that you think and act as they do. It's basic logic. Sit in a cold room, and you're going to get cold eventually. This is what happens as you spend time with your peer group or friends. You take on their patterns of belief and behavior, and they take on yours too. Ever heard the saying; "Iron sharpens iron?" Well, that's what's going on here. This could either be a really good thing or a really bad thing.

You have to think strategically when it comes to choosing your friends. You need to be mindful of your social circle. Do not assume for a second that you are completely immune to the effects that your friends can have on your life.

If you're doing something about stopping the drinking problem you suspect you're developing, then it doesn't make sense to hang out with people who basically bathe in alcohol all day and all night, does it? I'm not saying you should cut out all your friends who drink, merely that you would cut down on contact, or you would make sure you only ever hang out in places neither of you can get access to liquor.

In the process of achieving mastery, if you notice that you have friends who are anything but supportive, then bring out those big old scissors and get to snipping. It's either your so-called friends or your mastery of your craft. Which would serve your life better? You choose.

The fact is you cannot change other people unless they want to change. However, you can change the crowd that you choose to hang out with. In fact, it would be in your best interests to have friends who are determined to make something of them and take action every day to make it happen.

A study conducted in 2015 by the HSE Centre for Institutional Studies showed that over 100 Russian students performed at the same level as their friends, academically. It wasn't that they chose their friends on account of their grades, though. It just turned out that those who hung out with students who were high achievers did better in their own academic performance.

The right friends will assist you with self-control. When you're tempted to quit or tempted to do things that would derail your goal of ultimate mastery, your friends can be of help. A series of studies carried out by Duke University psychological scientists showed that for people who have low self-esteem, they stand much better chances of fighting the temptations when they have friends who are strong-willed. In other words, if you need help staying on track, then you must seek out friends and peers whose goals align with yours. You must seek out the sort of friends who have a backbone and are able to say no to distractions. These friends will help you find the strength you need inside of you to succeed in life.

I would be remiss if I didn't talk about the flip side of friendship a bit more. There are times when it's the people who are really close to you that are secretly pulling you down, whether it's a glass-totally empty coworker always complaining about one thing or the other, or the friend who is a total slob and won't get his crap together. So, you need to take inventory of your friends. Who is dragging you down? Who makes you feel like life is a crap fest? Who makes you feel your dreams are impossible to achieve? Figure that out.

Tim Ferris says you are the sum total of the 5 people you spend the most time with. I believe that is true, wholeheartedly, having had to make some tough decisions regarding some friends I had in the past myself. The older you get, the more you start to notice when your friends no longer have the same drive and ambition they used to. They are full of excuses for why they can't go after their dreams. This kind of constant chatter can be very bad for your psyche and will definitely hold you back from achieving mastery.

It's not liked your friends are intentionally holding you back all the time. It's just that they can project their own beliefs and limitations onto you, and if you're not careful, you will accept it. Sometimes they do this because they realize if you go after what you want and you succeed, then there's a chance they will have lost you for good.

You should make friends who are more successful than you are. Say you and your friends currently earn $40,000 per year, and you desire to add an extra zero to that figure. Does it sound reasonable to go ask your $40,000 a year buddies how to get that extra income? Of course not. Say you want to get more healthy and fit. Does it make sense to ask people who deliberately let themselves go and refuse to do anything about it how to lose weight? I want to believe you're smart, and you answered no to both of those questions.

You must find friends whose goals align with yours. If you live somewhere you can't find anyone who aspires to greatness, then don't worry. You've got the internet and amazing groups that can keep you on track. You've got podcasts you can listen to, books you can read or speakers who you can listen to, and so on. Use what you learn from them to grow into the person you'd like to be. Sure, you're going to be alone for a bit, unless your friends join you on your journey to mastery, but I've already mentioned before that the top is very lonely. The journey can be just as lonely, too, sometimes.

I have to be frank with you: Just because you and so-and-so have been best friends for over a decade doesn't mean you have to remain that way for the rest of your life. What are you, married to failure? If that best friend of yours is an anchor, let them go now. You will get a lot of backlashes, but I promise it's all going to be worth it. You need to be as strong as you can be and surround yourself with the right people who will help you achieve your goals. In the long run, you need a chance to make your dreams real. So, get rid of the anchors and get yourself friends that give you wings. You know, like a certain bull that's red in color. Only healthier.

Mentors matter because they keep you inspired. If you check in with anyone you know who is doing well in their career, they talk about mentors who have inspired them and given them golden, sage advice to follow, whether in person, or on the internet, or in a book. The thing about mentors is that their stories can keep us willing to continue with our pursuit of excellence. They have also made more than enough mistakes, so that you don't have to repeat them, but learn from their experience. It's basically like having the cheat codes to the video game of your craft

Another good reason you should find a mentor is that often, they can let you know when you need to sit up and do better. It's much better to take constructive criticism from your mentor versus your boss. You look up to your mentor. You trust your mentor. You don't have to deal with such petty things as workplace fights or resentments, which make it incredibly hard for you to really get what your superior is trying to teach you.

There's no one I know of who enjoys being told that they need to do better, or that they've done something wrong in the first place. However, when it comes from your mentor, who's an objective and detached third party, you can stomach the criticism better, and you'll actually be driven to do much better.

Mentors happen to have something that matters more than money: Relationships. If you do incredibly well, your mentor is going to want to connect you to those who will help you take your craft or career to the next level. This tends to be a natural occurrence because if there's anything your successful mentor likes doing, it's making meaningful connections — and that includes you if you distinguish yourself with your passion, commitment, and results.

Your mentor knows exactly what you need in order to achieve the mastery you seek. It's really no big secret: Work. Persistent patient work. When you're in the process of spending long, sleepless nights trying to get better, and you think that you couldn't possibly give any more of yourself, a message from your mentor could help to remind you that they were once in your shoes, and that's how they got where they are. They could even let you know that at this point, with all their success, they are still in your shoes. This can go a long way to inspire you. Your mentor will let you know the trillion number of times all they got was a door slam, an unreturned message, or some other variant of the word no. Yet, they were able to achieve what they achieved, which means you can, too, in spite of all the odds against you.

Chapter 13:

Plan your Time

Managing your time effectively is an important part of self-discipline. If you are unable to manage your time properly, you will not be able to accomplish the goals that you wish to complete in life and work. Time management is something that most people are taught in school. However, it is often not taught to them efficiently, and those that fail can contribute their failure to lack of time management. By putting pleasure above workload, you are creating an imbalance with your time management strategy. This means that you are using instant gratification as your driving force instead of long-term gratification. Those that are in balance will experience greater happiness, less stress, and more financial freedom.

Time management is the act of prioritizing the tasks that you must do in a schedule that is specific and calculated. Several mistakes are made by those that fail at time management. Each one of these mistakes is listed below with details on how it will affect your life. I have also included ways to combat these failures.

Not Maintaining a List of to-Dos

There are many times that I would stare off into space, and my kids would ask me what is wrong. Only for me to reply with, "I feel like I forgot something." Have you ever experienced this? If so then you will understand what I mean about the value of a well thought out to-do list. The to-do list helps to organize the day. It provides a schedule of events and a timeline of what one needs to accomplish today, this week, and this month. Without a to-do list, one would have this conversation with their kids daily. If you are experiencing moments of forgetfulness, then you should invest in the time it takes to make a to-do list.

When you do not use your to-do list to accomplish your goals, you place yourself at risk of failure as well as, disappointment. The most effective way to use a to-do list is to prioritize the things that are on your list

By breaking down all the things, you need to do into smaller, much simpler tasks you can have a less overwhelming time management tool. An example of this would be to write down the steps that it would take to write your first novel. However, this can seem huge. So instead, underneath this title, you will need to write down things like:

- Designate the set characters.
- Chose the location.
- Chose the book's theme.
- Decide on the plot for each character.
- Decide on the title for the book.
- Research the culture of the characters, the background, the language, the behaviors, and mannerisms.
- Build an outline that encompasses all things into it.
- Build a synopsis that will explain the storyline.
- Write the first chapter.

These are just a few of the steps that you would need to break down into much smaller steps. This will give you a less overwhelming and more accurate idea of what is necessary for the writing of a novel.

Personal Goals Have Not Been Set

Your personal goals pertain to the goals that are specific to your needs and your desires for the future. So, what is it that you want to do in the next year? What about the next five years? You can take this even further and determine what you want to do in the next ten years. This will help you to schedule your time wisely so that you can begin to build upon your goals.

This is an essential part of managing your time and building a foundation for your future. To reach your destination, you will need to have a vision of what you want. This vision will help you to make small achievable steps to accomplish all the things that need to be done to get you to the result.

By setting goals for each one of these categories, you will be able to build a foundation for discipline and goal setting that is sustainable.

Not Scheduling your Tasks by Priority

It is extremely hard to understand prioritizing the tasks that you have in a proper and functional manner. If you are currently working on an important task, then you need to stay focused and not allow distractions to interfere with your train of thought. This means if something comes up that is not life or death, and then stay focused and determined not to be sidetracked. Then when you are done, you will be able to handle the situation that arose while working. This allows you to show priority to the things that are most important at that time.

False emergencies will arise throughout your day; the key is to prioritize properly so that you do not allow distractions to interfere in your workday progress. Not all things will need to be immediately started or accomplished; some things can be put off till a better time presents itself. So, consider what the most important task is and finish that before being distracted by other things that are less important.

By prioritizing the tasks that you need to do, you are learning how to manage your time efficiently. This can lead to a more concise and steadier schedule. Determining what is most important for completion within your workday is crucial to accomplishing the tasks at hand. Place those things that are most important within prominent spots on your schedule and at times that you are most alert and energized. This will ensure that you have completed the important work first and then you can tackle the other work in a systematic order.

Set a Priority for all your Projects Wisely

Prioritizing the steps that you need to take is crucial to know what to start on. This can be done by following this simple tutorial on prioritization. Start by categorizing the steps into 4 categories:

1. Important tasks that are urgent ones.
2. Important tasks that are not urgent ones.
3. Urgent tasks that are not important.
4. Tasks that are not urgent as well as, not important.

An important task that is urgent would be something that you would need to have done right away. A task that is important which has no urgency is a task that appears especially important but does not necessarily need to be completed right this second. An urgent task that is not important is one that is super important to complete but once completed creates extraordinarily little impact. Then you have the tasks that are not urgent or important. These tasks are super low on the priority scale and only offer the illusion that they are busywork. These can be done later.

Learn to Say "no" More Often

"NO" is a super hard thing to tell others, especially when you can see they are clearly in need. But sometimes it is for your own good that you say "no" to others when they try to overload you with tasks that would otherwise be completed by them. Many people will try to get you to help them, especially if you cannot say "no." If you start to say "no" more often, be prepared to piss some people off. They will find that you are selfish, simply because you will not do the things they should be doing for themselves.

Plan your Strategy Before Instilling it

One of the worst things that you can do is immediately start your workday without a plan which is clear regarding what has to be completed for the day. The time that you are spending on the pre-thought process about the tasks you need to complete is trivial in comparison to the time you would be losing by jumping from one task to another without finalizing the first one. This creates a pattern of failing to complete projects before starting another one. Consider attempting one of the techniques listed below if you experience this: The night before, clear your desk and your mind of that day's work activities.

Let the Distractions Which Interfere in your Day Be Completely Eliminated

Begin to pay close attention to those times that others are more distracting throughout your workday. Track any interruptions that are induced by yourself — especially those that tend to be of the social media type. Your smartphone can be an extremely helpful device to have; however, the smartphone is additionally an addictive device.

It will take an exercise in self- discipline to shut out the distractions that can be causing loss of focus on your tasks. This limits your ability to maintain the proper focus that is needed to complete your work. Eliminate immediate access to smartphones, the internet, and outside communication with others. This helps you to maximize the productive time that you are spending in work mode. Rather than living as if you are "always on," set up an opportunity within the day to catch up on incoming email, contacting clients back, speaking with employees, and all the other distracting activities that derail your progress.

Delegate the Tasks that you Cannot Do to someone Else More Times Than not

If you have diligently hired the right and most talented employees, then you should have a dedicated and hard-working staff. This will help you get much of the work checked off of the to-do list, once you start to delegate the assignments. Managing a smaller business can depend on your abilities to maintain faith in your employees, and the ability to trust that the tasks will be completed appropriately and on time. This limits your involvement in the operation of each said task without having to delegate or micro-manage each person. Exploring every opportunity, delegating business responsibilities is a great way to maintain your workload and show the team that you trust their judgment and work ethics. This also increases morale and pride in their work.

Keep Track of your Productive Hours and the Time that you Spend Focused on one Single Task

How many minutes per week are you cramming in productive work? By using an easy to fill out a timesheet, you will be able to identify the moments that you are productive and the moments that you are not. This allows you to have a quick in and out the process for clocking your time. This also allows you to process the varied tasks that are in your day. Note down the jobs done for each day with a process that allows you to record the steps that you took and empty your mind of the tasks that you just completed. This opens your mind for the coming tasks without any hindrance or distraction. You can utilize a mobile app, or a written time tracking system that is directly connected to your desktop. This will give you the ability to have reports of your time spent in each task as well as, examine the productivity that you have had overall in your day, week, and month. This is also a great way to track the time of your employees as well.

Conclusion

While it is hard to find faults within ourselves about what we had done wrong in the past that shapes our future activities, rather we point a finger at the faults of others and neglect that our four fingers are in fact pointing at us. I have simply done the opposite. I am not pointing fingers at anyone for my mistakes.

In this guidebook – Skills for investing money - it does not tend to provide all the answers you ever wanted to start your new business ventures from scratch. Some of the business projects or steps I had taken to resolve my own business issues came from actually doing them, such as crafting official letters and communicating strategically to stakeholders. In other words, I did not cross the bridge until I got there.

However, what I can only assure you is this: You are not alone in your journey to establishing your profitable business. Do not be afraid to take business risks. Previous failures should not deter you from translating your new ideals into businesses that create employment for other people.

Rather, the fact that risks and failures collide like rockets, stars, and huge rocks in the warfare of your mind should be the motivating factors for you to stop thinking, and start acting to creating some nice, profitable business ventures from scratch in your local community.

As an entrepreneur and a business leader, what is common among businesses is the cash flow. Provided you keep your cash flow healthy, just like you do when you go to the gym once a week to shape your fitness, so must you keep your finances fit. You cannot spend what you do not have. Planning and budgeting are some of the key principles of financial success.

What you have read so far in this guidebook are some of the strategies I deployed to drive my businesses forward. What I learned in the MBA classroom, sometimes did not make any sense in the classroom, but became sensible when I applied them in my day-to-day job activities.

I had failed more than a hundred times to achieve business success. What matters most in life is what you do with the lessons or knowledge you learned from your failures. Life will not wait for you. By trying some tasks repeatedly, and failing them repeatedly, eat a humble pie, and learn from them. Your education is a waste of money and your time if what you learned at College or University does not solve a problem for society. Do not be afraid to follow your passion, to create your own work, be your own boss, and create jobs for others. You do not have to start big. Just start your dream business with the smallest amount you can afford – just anything. Remember that the youngest millionaires of today did not start big. They started small but ended up big in million pounds GBP revenue. The only obstacle stopping you from achieving true success is YOU. You need three things to succeed, namely, YOU, Courage, and Determination.

Whatever the situation, never be afraid to follow your passion by starting your business from scratch and also thank you for choosing this guidebook.

www.ingramcontent.com/pod-product-compliance
Lightning Source LLC
Chambersburg PA
CBHW071408210526
45465CB00001B/301